"I became acquainted wit
but I didn't get to know h
years, both of us attending .... church at Louisiana Downs. We have been friends through many life-changing events – living with autism, death, and cancer to name a few. She is one of the most tenacious and dedicated ladies I have ever known, and tenacity is evident in all her pursuits, whether it is seeking a deeper and more complete relationship with our Savior, Jesus Christ, learning to live with and through autism, or her latest conquest, writing a book. She tackled this book in true Lisa-fashion, with the Holy Spirit right by her side, guiding her through the entire process. I am so honored to call this lady one of my dearest and closest friends and to be Devin's 'Grandma Two'."

— ANN M. KENNINGTON,
Vice President, Ministry Team at Winner's Circle Church

"This book will be a breath of fresh air to *all* mothers and fathers who are raising special-needs children and will give a new revelation to those who desire a closer walk with God. It is easy to read and will capture your attention as I could not lay it down until the last page. After reading it, I felt God's presence as never before and knew… the Lord is my strength, refuge, and is always present in time of need. Thank you, Lisa, for reminding me how God puts miracles in my life every day!"

— JACKIE SWANK,
Mary Kay Independent National Sales Director Emeritus

"My definition of Lisa Pappas Perrodin: amazing, beautiful, resilient, compassionate, brave, determined, honest, courageous, intelligent, loving, but most of all… she has that rare and special gift from God that she shares with everyone. She is a blessing to all she encounters. I am thankful that she has shared her gift with us and that she came into our lives 32 years ago! We are truly blessed and refer to both her and Devin as our family. Love you both always!"

—CHERI DELAHOUSSAYE,
Owner, Dela LLC and C & P Properties LLC

Walking with God through Autism is an amazing story of a young boy and his adventures through 12 years of life. It will make you laugh, pray, and cry at his innocence. It will teach you as it grips your heart. So, settle in as you begin because, if you're like most people, you won't put it down until the last page."

—BEVERLY LEWIS,
Community Angels of Hope

"From the very first chapter, I could not put this book down, nor could I stop thinking about it. *Walking with God through Autism* will definitely stay in your heart. Lisa is a very talented writer, and I believe that there will be many more life stories from her to come."

—SUSAN BRANDON ALLEN,
Director of Administrative Services

"I've known the Perrodin family for a couple of decades. Through them, I have witnessed a change that can only be described as supernatural. In a career as competitive as horseracing, we still consider ourselves as family... sharing victories and heartaches as well. It has been an inspiration to watch such courage in their walk through life with Christ."

—SHANE J. SELLERS,
Former National Thoroughbred Jockey

"I have known Lisa Pappas Perrodin for many years. I was extremely honored when she asked me to review this book. Now, after reading it, I am left almost speechless by how lovingly she wrote about her 'walk through the fire' of autism with God. Her son, Devin, was a very young boy when I first met this family. My connection with them began when her husband, E.J. Perrodin, raced at The Fairgrounds Racetrack in New Orleans. I got to be their chaplain here at this track. Friend, I know that, like me, when you pick up this book and begin reading, it will be hard to put down until you read through the final chapter. I can't wait for it to be available to all as it is truly life changing."

—CHAPLAIN WAVERLY PARSONS,
The Fairgrounds Racetrack, New Orleans, Louisiana
Past President, The Racetrack Chaplaincy of America

"Dentistry for children with autism violates every condition associated with the disorder: strangers, close confinement, new surroundings, different loud noises, things in one's mouth that can create startling sounds and vibrations, etc. I have observed Devin evolve from terrified and obstinate, into a totally cooperative young person. He now looks forward to our visits for hygiene and routine maintenance. This behavioral change goes beyond good… it is from God. In this book, you will see how prayer is put into action. It reveals the unexplained, not in our way, but in God's Way… for His glory. This is a 'must read' for all!"

—DR. ERIC J. LEBLANC,
Pediatric Dentist with One-Year Fellowship at
Johns Hopkins in Dentistry for Children with Special Needs

"This well written, heart-wrenching, transparent journey of an amazing autistic boy, and his deeply loving, self-sacrificing mother captured my heart. As a writer, educator, and life coach, I believe this book relates to every person who has been bombarded by life experiences… that tempt them to wonder, 'Why Me?' This book is not only riveting, but also, victorious."

—FRANCES DURON,
Co-Founder, Shreveport Community Church and
Evangel Christian Academy

Walking with
GOD
through
AUTISM

Lisa Pappas Perrodin

High Bridge Books
Houston

DEDICATION

This book is wholeheartedly dedicated to my Lord and Savior, Jesus Christ. His sacrifice has made the way for my salvation.

Secondly, to my loving son, Devin. It is he who led me into this close relationship with God. My son is the greatest gift my Heavenly Father has entrusted to me. He used Devin's exceptionalities as beautiful, primary tools in bringing me closer to the Lord. And because of this, I now trust my amazing Father in all that I do.

Contents

Acknowledgements

Special thanks go out to those who the Lord specifically has placed in our lives.

Our family, friends, therapists, teachers, and church family... have all been such a blessing to us.

Also, we are eternally grateful for our amazing supporters: Chaplain Jimmy Sistrunk, who started paving our walk with God; Winner's Circle Church Ministry team and members; Northpoint Community Church; Shreveport Community Church; as well as our families throughout the entire horse racing industry, including their chaplains and staff as well. You have all stood behind us in prayer, believing in agreement for every miracle that God has bestowed on us.

I love and cherish each of you… more than you'll ever know!

INTRODUCTION

When we come into this world, we have no idea what life has in store for us. We can't choose our parents, environment, or the unique characteristics that mold us into either who we are or who we will become. Our culture and the immediate world around us quickly put us into a specific place. We begin to grow, wearing blinders and only seeing the path directly in front of us.

There is a God, however, who uniquely knitted you together within your mother's womb. He knew you before she ever thought of conceiving you. He knew your story before you began to write the first page. He had plans for you that were greater than anything you could possibly have imagined.

He is your biggest fan, your unfailing Father, and your best friend. We may not all recognize Him in the beginning, but time and circumstances will give you the opportunity to make Him a part of your life. And then, when you choose to let Him in, you will see how everything around you will change.

This is my story, my testimony, and my personal account of the amazing love that God has for us. It is proof that what the world may see as undesirable our Heavenly Father sees as blessing. This book is for all the mothers who question why they have been given a special needs child for whom to care. It is a reminder that you did not do anything wrong to deserve this challenge but that you are blessed to have been entrusted with such an important responsibility. You will discover through reading this book that God is all-loving and that He will help you grow to become a more amazing person than you ever dreamed you could become.

There are many sorrows through which we must walk. There are hundreds of bumps in the road. Yet, there are also rainbows and promises that God gives to us in His Word. It is by holding on to and trusting in His Word that true faith begins. Through that faith, we find true peace and comfort.

God not only gave an incredibly gifted son to me, but He also allowed this child's struggles to bring me to my knees. Feeling like one sinking deeper and deeper into a pit of quicksand, I was brought to the end of my rope. Panic and frustration grew to a point of breaking, and hope became a lost word in my vocabulary. It became a job just to get out of bed in the mornings.

Yet, in the midst of my battle, I formed a relationship with my Creator that is now secure and permanent. I am proud to say that I was led to God through autism. I am reborn. Though I have a long way to go, I am now a smarter, stronger, and more-loving person than I ever dreamed possible.

As we are moving forward, filled with joy and continuing to grow, God is walking right beside us through it all.

1

MY WORLD THROUGH TINTED GLASSES

"Like newborn babies, you must crave pure spiritual milk so that you will grow into a full experience of salvation. Cry out for this nourishment, now that you have had a taste of the Lord's kindness."

—1 PETER 2:2-3

On a cool and crisp September day, I came into this world. I was healthy, happy, and ready to begin my life with people who were exuberant about my arrival. My mother and father were a joyful couple, and my sister and brother (who were much older than I) were equally excited about my birth. It was as if the whole world revolved around me and only me.

There is always a beautiful newness that comes with the arrival of a baby. All who take part in that child's life know there is a change about to take place. Nothing will ever again be the same. I was to make a meaningful difference in each of them, and they would do the same in me. How could any child not feel totally complete with that much love?

We were a middle-class family. We lived by decent moral standards. We didn't attend church very often, but that did not mean our belief in God and Jesus was diminished in any way.

My father worked very hard for a living. He started his own business, and we watched as it grew and thrived. Yes, we had some hard times but not like many others I have come to know. There was always food on our table, clothing on our backs, and a roof over our heads.

My mother was not required to work and would always be there to nurture and care for us. At such an early age, I took this for granted. Today, most mothers must work in order to barely make ends meet.

As I grew, life continued quite well for me. I went to good schools, had great friends, and seemed to excel at almost everything I set out to do. I was not a boastful child. I simply thought this was typical for everyone. I believed, as long as you tried very hard to accomplish things, nothing could stop you from reaching those goals. Perhaps, this was a fantasy. On the other hand, maybe it was a trait God had planted in my mind prior to my birth.

As I grew, I discovered more about who I really was and what was in store for me. People and places were etched into my heart as my life became a map of accomplishments, trials, and failures. As my highways of life were being constructed, they seemed to be laid out on firm, solid ground.

I don't recall being around kids who were physically or mentally challenged. I was either preoccupied with my own agenda or blind to the things I did not want to see.

My life had taken on a persona somewhat akin to a fairytale character. In academics, I maintained honor-roll status. My achievements in sports were quite impressive. I had no problem getting what I wanted. I worked hard at reaching many victories, and they were attained quite easily. Getting boyfriends was never a problem. I was likeable, witty, and attractive to most of my friends and acquaintances. This also made my interactions with others more productive. Everything seemed to fall into place so nicely. My family had always supported my efforts, and I was immensely showered with love and favor.

Throughout this period in my life, I gave credit for my success to my parents and retained a significant portion of praise for my own personal efforts. I did not realize that it was God who was pouring out His favor on me. As easy as it is to appreciate Him now, it was most difficult then.

Throughout high school, things continued to move along quite easily... maybe, too easily. I was no longer being challenged the way I wanted to be, and I was becoming bored with the good things in life. Looking for something else to fill an emptiness that still remained inside, I experimented with drugs. That experimentation didn't last very long.

I decided to marry as soon as I finished high school. I needed to break away and become independent. My merry life was now about to change because of bad judgments and hasty, impulsive choices. I wanted to grow up in a hurry and learn how to take care of myself. Like most adults, I wanted to work in the real world and increase my sense of self-worth. I thought I was ready to dive into the bigger and better things awaiting me. Sound typical? I guess it was.

I had been the typical teenager, thinking I had the answers to everything. I was even sure that I had the solution for world peace. That much energy, attitude, and raw enthusiasm can be dangerous if not directed in an appropriate manner. I desired to do the right things; however, I had no spiritual leader to guide me. I was about to embark on a journey along which my decisions and actions would have certain consequences.

After my first marriage ended quickly, I went off to sow some wild oats. Although I had caused my own misery, I was feeling sorry for myself because I had missed out on going to college with my friends. Perhaps it wasn't too late to pick up the pieces of my life, but I still had not learned much from my recklessness.

I moved back home and got a fun and interesting job at the local horse track. It was there where my parents ran the racehorses they owned. I started making up for lost time with my old friends and acquaintances. Life was grand. I was free, safe, and thinking this was going to satisfy my appetite. But I still had an emptiness lingering inside.

Where was my God? Why had He not come to my rescue after the horrible decision I had made in marriage? I needed His guidance. However, I had never gone to Him for such guidance. I never went to church. I never looked for the answers to my questions in the right places. I had been avoiding the things that I would ultimately be required to face. I did not want to face the truth.

There is no truth in living without boundaries and rules. There is no happiness found in anything this world has to offer. In trying to convince myself that there was, I was only living a lie.

The standard on which I chose to live my life was based on the principles of mathematics. I would use the principle of trial and error to arrive at my decisions. Those things which led to failure were crossed out and eliminated. The remainder of possibilities would be weighed and balanced before drawing any conclusions. This seemed to be a rational way to arrive at the answers to life's questions. I was trying to use practicality like a scientist would. Little did I know, this was just a waste of time.

I had no idea that my Creator possessed the answers to all my questions. I was making life more difficult than it had to be.

My reasoning and search for happiness then led me into a relationship with a professional athlete. He did not turn to God for answers any more often than I had. Though, it seemed to be an awesome time of love, partnership, and traveling. We went everywhere together. Growing closer to one another, we tackled all our fears with one mind. Both having made a mess of our first marriages by committing to the wrong people, neither of us wanted to get married again. We shared the same ideas about things, believed in the same values, and were skeptical when it came to making drastic changes.

Although these ways of looking at life brought us together, God knew what was best for us. He used that natural bond to turn us into better individuals with solid spiritual awareness. We struggled with uncertainty as to what tomorrow would hold, and we were convinced that our relationship was perfect.

One can never know nor appreciate what true happiness is until making a commitment to God. There will always be doubts that surface in one's mind from time to time. Though, nothing will ever satisfy a person more completely than the love of the Most High. His grace is sufficient and will carry you through every situation you face in life. He will be your strength in all of your weaknesses. Only God can complete you.

If you cannot accept this principle of life, you will be discouraged at every point. You will be critical of the things in your mate that are never enough. Their inadequacies will anger you because it will seem that you are being used. Rather than building one another up, there will be a strain on the bond that had once been formed.

Approaching a stagnant point in our life together, we agreed that a change was in order. It was clear the time had come to take things to the next level. We were getting older, so the possibility of growing as a family became more appealing. His career would eventually come to an end as is the case with all professional athletes. My body was getting older, and having never had a child, Mother Nature would be working against me.

So, having a child became our new plan. Life would advance into the next chapter. The journey ahead would take on new twists and turns. Some doors would be shut behind us, but new ones would soon be open. Were we being driven by bravery or mere foolishness? Who knows for certain? Our Lord knows. His plans for us were already taking on substance.

We married and put our family plans in the hands of God. If He meant for us to have a child, He would see to all the details. We had finally begun to ask for His help. Without even realizing it, our faith had become activated.

At times, we stumbled across His path, and He opened the door of change. It happened so we could be led in the right direction. That's what it took for us to follow God's lead. It was an almost unconscious call to follow our instincts and dare to face the unknown. By exhibiting moral behavior on our part, the realization of His presence became more acute. That, you see, is when and where my dear Father began to step into my life. It was by invitation only!

When you're young or not properly guided, it is so easy to become deaf to wisdom and truth. That is why many of life's challenges must be faced by some people more so than others. Either way, God loves all His children profusely and equally. He will never leave your side. And that is true, no matter how unworthy you may feel.

Years had passed without conception. I thought, "Maybe I'm not supposed to be a mother." Why should I be? I had no real experience with babies. I grew up thinking only of myself and what I wanted out of life. I would never babysit for the children of other parents. I had never offered and felt no guilt in denying anyone who thought of asking me. What provoked me to want children of my own?

Such were the doubts introduced to my mind by the enemy. He wanted to tear me apart with feelings of unworthiness, and that's true no matter what I was trying to achieve.

Where God works to produce your greater good, the devil continues to throw darts at your goals and objectives. By making me feel like I didn't deserve anything, he began the process of "robbing, killing, and destroying." He is a liar and a thief. Never underestimate his ability to deceive. He is the master at bringing pain, loss, and disaster to everyone. And now, I had left myself open to all of his massive attacks.

After giving up on attempts of trying to conceive on my own, I allowed God to step in and do whatever He had planned for me. And with that submission, I finally got pregnant. We were so excited that we could not help but tell everyone we knew. It was really going to happen. I would get to be a mother, and I could not wait to get started.

I prepared by picking out baby names, shopping for infant clothes, and doing all the wonderful things that went along with our baby's arrival.

My husband's career was booming beyond belief. Already an accomplished and successful jockey of thoroughbred race horses, everything was flourishing beyond our wildest dreams.

Trying to soothe our earlier pain of possible barrenness, we made plans to take a cruise. And though I was now pregnant, we continued with those previously made plans. I was in my late-30s at the time, but I took good care of myself. I didn't think that my age was anything for us to worry about concerning the pregnancy.

I had no problem tackling anything else I set my mind to do, but my confidence would be shaken most unexpectedly. There were lessons in humility that I had yet to learn.

Before leaving on the only vacation we had ever attempted, I started to hemorrhage slightly. To be sure that I and the baby were healthy, I went in to see my doctor and had an ultrasound preformed. He told me that I was not very far along and not to worry. There would be a doctor on board the ship if I needed one, so I should just take it easy. I was not to do too much.

Being excited about all the great things that were happening, I went worry free. The first three days passed without incident. However, I began feeling weaker as each day passed. I thought perhaps it was a combination of morning sickness and sea sickness. The bleeding persisted. I was scared to the point of panicking. I could hardly contain myself. Finally, we went to see the ship's doctor. I was now in non-stop pain. I knew it wasn't good.

The doctor confirmed my worst fears. I had lost the baby. The heavy bleeding was my body's way of cleaning out the remains. I had never before known of anyone who had miscarried, so this was a complete shock to me. Not only were we required to walk through this pain, we would walk through it again as we returned home to explain it all to family and friends.

It was hard enough trying to tell myself what had just transpired. The contracting pains had now moved from my abdomen to my chest and throat. I was trying not to cry, but the sorrow took control of me, leaving a bitter taste in my body and soul. My husband did not know what to say. He was as heartbroken as I.

Wanting to run away, we were out at sea, and there was no turning around until the ship completed its route as scheduled. We went back to the cabin, but I just wanted to be left alone. I was so deeply distressed, both physically and emotionally. I wanted to scream at God and ask why He would allow this to happen. What had I done so wrong? Was the attitude I had about children in my younger years bad enough to deserve this? I could not understand. I wanted someone to explain the justification for all of this pain. If I knew what I had done, I could correct it and make sure that it did not happen again.

The devil had me blaming myself for everything. I was fooled into thinking that my Father in Heaven was disappointed with me. Such unnecessary pain we put ourselves through when we are blind to God's love. He was with me through all of it and felt my pain with more compassion than my earthly father could ever give. God was pressing closer to me. But, in my disbelief, I could not feel His divine presence.

That night was one of my longest as we both curled up on the bed in silence, embracing one another. This was no vacation. This was no celebration. We accepted it as punishment for our immoral living arrangement prior to marriage.

There were only three days left until we would dock, and we spent them as though nothing had happened. I did not want to talk about it again but wanted to act as if I had never been pregnant. I would be required to tell my parents and friends when we got back, but for now, it was not up for discussion.

I would go forward, put this memory behind me, and start the healing process as quickly as possible. Neither being mad at God nor putting the blame on myself would be helpful. Neither strategy would return my baby to me. Such was the way I began dealing with my shattered life. I toughened my heart, picked up my head, and put one foot in front of the other.

Arriving home was something I dreaded. Not only would I be required to rehash the facts, but I would return to my doctor for tests.

Our family and friends were quite sympathetic to our loss. In fact and to my surprise, others seemed open to sharing their own miscarriage experiences. The doctor explained that perhaps something was wrong with the baby and that the miscarriage may have been God's way of protecting us from things that could have been far more painful. Even without medical help, my body was responding remarkably well, and I had become almost totally cleansed. We only had to wait a few months before trying again.

Convinced that this tragedy had occurred because of something I had done, the prospects were quite uncertain. My heart's desire was to confess anything and everything, hoping I would be made right with God before another attempt. So this was what I did.

As we traveled from place to place on the racing circuit, the memory of our loss was becoming easier to bear. We built our confidence to try again and got our second chance. This time, we were careful not to share our excitement before the actual event. If something went wrong again, it would be less traumatic if fewer people knew about it. My heart, likewise, would not be forced to endure the pain with each explanation.

We were very exuberant, and it was extremely difficult to hold back the good news, but we agreed to keep our secret under wraps through the first trimester. I was working at every track to which we traveled, and we had many friends scattered throughout the country. I was not showing, which made it easier to remain silent. But even in our silence, the enemy's distressing presence remained at the door of heart and soul. He wants to steal our joy whether we try to ignore him or not.

It was a very special day to us. We were racing on a beautiful Sunday afternoon that happened to be Mother's Day. It was a wonderful day of celebration for me as I used it to mark the beginning of a new era for me: Motherhood. Reminiscing about memories of my own mother, I was filled with an inner peace and tranquility that was more than satisfying.

However, breaking into the reverie of this beautiful day was a horrible accident. A horse had broken its leg in the middle of a race. It was in the lead, just in front of the others when it occurred. As the horse and rider fell abruptly to the ground, I watched as the rest of the horses trampled over them. My heart wrenched in my chest as I watched. I immediately grabbed the program to see who it was. It was my husband.

All wives of jockeys experience this awful nightmare at one time or another. It may be one's own husband who falls and is trampled. Such was the case for me this time. After seeing him hit the ground hard, I stared in shock as his own horse was tossed in the air and landed directly on him. Meanwhile, the other horses and riders trampled his frail, thin body. He laid motionless on the track after this horrific incident.

Almost immediately, the phone was ringing to alert my supervisor as to who was involved in the accident and to pass the word along to me. But the only ringing I heard was in my own head. It was a sickening pressure that was building in my mind and in my heart. My co-workers tried to help by reassuring me God would take care of everything. But deep inside, as I tried to believe them, doubts were growing.

I scurried down flights of stairs and raced my way to the ambulance below. Before they took him to the hospital, I needed to hear his voice and see for myself how badly he was injured. They were closing the doors, but I insisted they allow me to see him before they departed.

Conscious and able to talk, he was in a great deal of pain. He told me that he thought he had broken his back. They strapped him to a board to restrict his motion.

I followed them to the hospital, and continually prayed to God. I begged Him! If I had a choice in this matter, I would pick my husband over the baby. I had already experienced the loss of a baby. I wasn't ready to lose my husband. He was my best friend as well. I told the Lord I would accept His decision as long as I could keep my partner.

As most emergency room visits go, we had been there for hours before we knew anything. Numerous x-rays were taken with long waiting periods in between.

Finally, after a doctor appeared with the results, we were told that nothing was broken and that we could now return home.

Something, however, was not right. He remained in agony. Although they repeatedly assured us it was only pain from damaged muscles and tissue, he still could not stand or walk on his own. They got him into my car. After arriving back home, I practically had to carry him from my car into our trailer.

The long day—filled with trauma, panic, and stress—had begun to take its toll on me. But the final struggle to get him into the trailer and somewhat comfortable sent things over the top. As had happened before, I started bleeding. Trying to sleep, tears of agony welled up inside of me.

I was fairly sure of what was happening. The only difference this time was that I had cut a deal with God. I had bargained and agreed to accept the consequences for His help in return. Although my body was now hurting with pain, my heart was convinced that this was not a punishment. I was experiencing the results of divine negotiation and its consequences.

I called my doctor the first thing in the morning. She insisted I come to her office immediately.

After giving my husband some pain medication, I told him what was happening and that I would be back shortly.

Ultrasounds were taken. The results brought certainty to my expectations. I had lost my second child.

I made it clear to my doctor that I neither wanted nor needed any complex explanations for what had happened. I was certain in my heart of what had transpired and why. The only difference from the first loss was that, this time, I saw that motionless embryo floating inside of me… floating without a heartbeat. I witnessed the absence of life before my very eyes. And because of my choice, I painfully accepted the outcome.

It may have been easier for me to accept it this time but not for my husband. Guilt washed over him like a tidal wave. He felt responsible for it all, and there was not much I could do to help him get beyond it.

The following day, we took him to a specialist. There were, in fact, broken bones in his back. Some of the small bones that come out of the spine, holding the muscles securely in place, had been broken off with muscle tissue attached. This was not an injury requiring surgery. It would, however, require months for complete healing to be accomplished.

Once again, God had proven His faithfulness toward us. My perception and appreciation of Him appeared to be quite rational. However, I had no idea exactly how much the Lord truly loved us. My mind was certain that we had been helped by God by virtue of the sacrifice I had been willing to endure. Attributing grace to His precious love alone was beyond me. We had so much to learn about the depth and breadth of that amazing love. These were only baby steps leading us to something so much greater, a greatness our minds could not fathom.

2

STUMBLING INTO HIS LIGHT

"The teaching of Your word gives light, so even the simple can understand."

—PSALM 119:130

Each trial encountered with faith in God tends to bring people closer to His light. Some Christians who have a typical church-going background may be led into that light much more easily. For those of us who lived gypsy-like lifestyles, we stumble into God's light in order to gain a proper understanding of how much He cares for His children. For those who have never read the Bible, His Word and promises remain a mystery.

We survived unimaginable trials throughout our marriage. We were a brave pair with tough and deeply embedded survival instincts. What God had planned for us went far beyond normal limits and expectations.

We gave family planning a third attempt. Once again, we successfully planted a good seed. Our primary hope and goal was that it would remain planted. Having reached beyond the first trimester, we thought we were home free. However, the bleeding returned as before.

Both of us had been quite successful in our jobs. Everything appeared to be in perfect order. There seemed to be no reason for this to happen again. We thought our manner of life was pleasing to God. We were good people always faithful to help out the less fortunate. Trying so hard to be worthy of receiving this child, in our blindness, we missed the fact that our Lord simply desired a meaningful relationship with us.

We were to visit my doctor the next morning. An ultrasound was scheduled with the hope of hearing a heartbeat. I went to bed that night more restless than ever. I was unable to hold back the tears and didn't want to awaken my husband. At the end of my patience, I crawled up on the sofa in our den and delivered an ultimatum to God. My heart was broken, and I poured the pain out to Him. My Heavenly Father needed to hear that I was at my limit. I didn't want to experience this again. I needed an answer from Him that was clear and to the point. I would try no longer. It was going to be "three strikes and you're out" or "the third time's a charm."

I left the decision to Him. If I lost this child, I would have my tubes tied and cut. Should He allow me to have the baby, I was "all in"… no matter the cost. I would do my best to help this child learn as much about our Lord as possible. Such was my promise to God, and I declared it with all of my heart.

Morning came. My husband knew how distraught I must have been to find me on the couch when he awoke. He was trying to be strong, but I could see the anxiety on his face.

We quietly got ready and arrived at the doctor's office in silence. It seemed that the fear of the unknown had paralyzed both of us. As my doctor read the ultrasound and prepared to announce its results, my husband had already maneuvered himself into a corner of the room in preparation for bad news. I knew he was afraid that he could not be my strength this time around.

As she got started, the embryo could be seen clearly, and the heartbeat was detected.

My husband was still facing the wall like a scolded child who had been sent to the corner when the doctor turned up the volume as loud as the machine could go. That beautiful, rapid, and glorious sound filled the room. He had no idea what was going on until the doctor said, "Well, Dad… Are you going to turn around and look at your little boy or what?"

As he turned to see the smiles on our faces, tears were pouring down his weathered cheeks. He was at the screen, lightly touching the image. In total shock, he said, "Really, Doc? Is this definitely his heartbeat? And are you sure that we're having a boy?" Our smiles could not match the glory of the miracle we both were witnessing.

She told us that the baby's sex was not yet known. It was still too early to be detected.

"But, if I were the wagering kind," she said, "My gut instinct bets that it's a boy. Yes! A boy with a *very* big heart!"

We left her office on a cloud. It was a cloud sent from Heaven by God Himself. His answer was quite simple and clear. His promise was sealed within my heart as was mine in His. This was going to be my special gift. Whether it was earned or not, it didn't matter. I was already on a path leading to His wonderful light.

Giving God an ultimatum may sound extremely bold, but this is how personal relationships develop from time to time. Putting yourself out on a limb with another individual is how we grow and develop bonds of trust. It also builds a person's character. I had yet to learn this, but I was only ready to receive small portions at a time.

After this unforgettable turn in our lives, pregnancy was a breeze. There was no morning sickness, and I glowed like an angel. Never in my life had I ever been more healthy or fit.

When it was time to find out the sex of our child, sure enough, that doctor had been correct. We had a boy.

Subsequent ultrasounds were incredible. He was bouncing around in my belly like a racehorse. His heartbeat stayed strong, and he was growing as a normal, healthy baby should. My son and I were united from the moment I could actually feel him within me. Many nights, as he grew larger, I would run my finger slowly across my stomach, and he would follow it with either his hand or foot. Carrying him was incredible. He was embedded in my body and soul. I was somewhat afraid that, after delivery, the closeness would change. I feared that those personal moments between us may become lost in a sea of memories.

I knew my husband had bonded with his son the moment he heard that heartbeat and touched the screen. I saw the love in his eyes and began to realize that the Heavenly Father's love for His children had to be even deeper.

The moment came to give birth just one day after his due date. I was scared, but my husband's trust in the Lord was a bit deeper than mine. He was ready to be my coach and to help me bring this wonderful miracle of ours into the world.

At that point, however, things became a bit more complicated. As I was moving into strong labor, the baby was not dropping as he should have. I was not dilating a centimeter. Hours were passing. My primary physician was out of town, and no one could seem to find his backup.

I was 41 years old and having my first baby. I was not willing to risk losing him at any cost. I had agreed and already signed the papers to have a caesarian delivery if that were to be necessary. But no one was there to help me with the delivery.

In the room next to ours, a woman delivered twins, but only one had survived. It appeared to me, even amidst my own labor, that the entire floor was rather chaotic. Waves of labor pain washed over and exhausted me. We were already nine grueling hours into labor before I finally got an epidural.

The following morning, the backup doctor arrived. He wanted to break my water and induce labor once again. I was so tired that I just wanted them to get my baby out before something bad happened to him. All of his vitals were still stable.

When I looked at my husband, asking him what to do, he said, "We've trusted God this far. I think your gut instinct is *Him* speaking to you. Let's just do the C-section and get our boy out safely. Your mind's already made up. Don't let these guys change it." That was probably the greatest advice my husband had ever given to me.

I told them I did not care if they had to slice me in the sign of the cross. I told them to just get my baby out before he suffocates or something worse. Although the doctor was not too happy about it, he ordered another chest-down epidural. Sadly, my husband could only be with me briefly during this surgery. He would not be able to enjoy the pleasure of cutting the cord. Our boy's safety was his concern, first and foremost. As our son was being lifted from my womb, I could only see the fearful look on my husband's face. The umbilical cord was wrapped several times around his little neck. Quickly, the doctor unwound it, and the tension in the room eased. A wonderful cry filled the room, and I knew that all was well. As my husband brought him to my face, I was greeted with the most beautiful smile.

After they had put my guts back into place, everyone but the surgeon left the room. He was quite snippy and rude as he stated, "Now, everything is going to center around that baby. You will feel completely alone." I smiled at him and said, "I don't care!" It was always about my little boy from day one. I wouldn't have had it any other way. I said, "Just make sure you don't forget to put one of my important parts back in, and I'll be just fine."

My Lord made good on His promise, and I was more than happy to fulfill my end of the bargain. That baby had us praying more and asking for God's intervention at every opportunity. He was the gift that brought us closer into the light of our Father's presence.

But while basking in the comfort of His peace, the devil was waiting. With critical timing, he sought to tear us away from God's fellowship. Our son's growth and maturity seemed to be on track for a child just under two years old. Though, it took him longer to crawl, to walk, and barely to talk.

The pediatricians explained it this way. Our son was the only baby in a house with much older parents than typical families. His slower development could be explained by over nurturing, especially because there was no other child around. He was probably not being pushed enough, they reasoned.

I guess their assessment made sense. My experience in these things was definitely limited. After all, they were the professionals. So, we worked harder at urging our son to do more while, at the same time, showering our little blessing with all the love and affection we had to give.

As our son, Devin, had already reached walking age, the next developmental hurdle was talking. Most children have begun to make an effort by this time, but it was not happening for our little boy. A pattern was developing and taking shape. Devin was lining up his toys in a certain order. It was an order only important to him. Eye contact was becoming less frequent, and his focus was always on something insignificant to the rest of the world. Walking on the tips of his toes was constant.

Ignoring the obvious, we remained passive when it came to passing judgement on our miracle. Some people would say that we should have gotten his hearing checked. After all, it may have been that he simply could not hear us when we would speak to him. That would surely be a reason for his limited speaking skills. However, Devin would respond to delicate sounds that interested him, even when his back was turned. His hearing was more acute to some things that even we did not hear. My husband would get angry if I tried to convince him that something was not right with our little boy. He was in more denial than I.

At that point, my father became ill. He was a strong man who was always staying busy with work. Nevertheless, his doctors discovered that a cold he could not shake was actually cancer. Tests were done, and each came back to the verdict: Stage 4. He had been a smoker for most of his life. Without regular check-ups, all symptoms had remained undetected or were silently covered up until it was too late. It started in his lungs and progressed throughout the rest of his body. They were not able to suggest any therapy of chemo or radiation at that point.

My brother lived closest to my dad and was able to help with the business more than my sister or I. We were living about six hours away but would come as often as possible to help them out.

During the remainder of his life, which spanned a little over a year, the entire family had also been devastated with severe personal loss due to Hurricane Katrina. It was like a non-stop sequence of horrific events. Devin's problems appeared so insignificant when compared to what the rest of the family was experiencing. We were more than happy to delay further testing. Trying to help with hurricane recovery took away quality time we could enjoy as a family unit.

Not long after rebuilding from the severe damage, it became apparent that my father's time was running out. Devin and I made a weekend visit to see my parents. It was obvious that we were near the end of Dad's suffering.

I had brought my Bible with me and asked my father if I could pray for him. He nodded yes. His voice had been reduced to a mere whisper. He had always been a non-believer, and I certainly was not skilled at final bedside speeches. Frightened and with my dependent son in hand, I asked God to be with us and to give me whatever it took to bring my dad to Himself. I then asked my dad to open up his heart and allow me to be the vessel between him and the Lord. I tried simply to function as a mediator between my earthly father and my Father in Heaven. Though God used me, I give credit to the Holy Spirit for His divine intervention throughout.

It was growing darker, and I did not want to turn on the light. The only part of the Bible I could remember was Psalm 23: "The Lord is my shepherd." I repeated that chapter over and over again until dad took his final breath. During his passing, I discovered that, when you do something pleasing for your Heavenly Father, He will shed a whole new light on your understanding. It's *His* brilliant light.

At the funeral, I spoke briefly with the hospice chaplain who performed the service. He had visited my dad during those final weeks, so I shared with him the events that happened on that final night and how heavy my heart had been concerning dad's faith.

That chaplain was my God-send. He informed me that Psalm 23 was my dad's favorite portion of the Bible. It seemed to pierce my father's heart to such an extent that he could relate to David in that very chapter. I thought I would hit the floor. I knew then that the Lord was not only my

Rock but that He loved me enough to respond during my hour of need. He did so through a total stranger. My Heavenly Father had been with me all along.

Returning home, I had an inexplicable thirst that was beginning to grow within me. I wanted to know more. My desire was to be filled until I overflowed with His presence. I had only scratched the surface of something I desperately needed in my life. I spoke more often with our racetrack chaplain than ever before, asking so many questions that I was surely driving him crazy.

I did not attend church, but I did go back to reading the Bible. Unsure concerning my son's problems, I knew God would not let me down. Furthermore, I believed with all my heart that the Lord would help me hold up my end of the bargain made with Him. I promised to be the best mom I could be no matter what circumstances came my way. And as I went deeper into God's Word, His promises to stand by me came more and more to life. I had a better understanding of things, but still there remained so much more to learn.

Our pediatrician agreed that it was time to have further testing done on Devin. The decision-making process provoked many arguments between my husband and me. He was still in denial that there was a problem and used as many excuses as possible to prove me wrong.

Screening was done regarding Devin's hearing problems, but when a child is non-verbal, results are more difficult to assess. Our son was displaying extreme outbursts with loud noises, separation from me, and anxiety over anything that set his world in disarray. I was becoming the monster in the family because everyone thought that I was exaggerating all of the symptoms.

Our marriage was becoming strained by the testing and its effects on Devin. His behavior was becoming worse, and my husband was convinced that it was entirely my fault. Not only were we drifting apart, we were also drifting away from God. I thought this was something I could fix and that all of our problems would go away.

Six months after my father's death and subsequent to a long regimen of testing, I was told that Devin's problem was autism. There is a range or spectrum for measuring this disorder. Parents can discover at what point their child is on that scale and how much help can be provided. Devin's condition put him at the end of *moderate to severe*. I was told he would surely require special care for the rest of his life and probably an institution as he grew older.

I was devastated by the report and could hardly believe what I was hearing. As the news was given to me, it was as though a dagger had been plunged into my heart. The dagger, more than likely, would have been less painful. I could barely cry because all I wanted to do was throw up. My insides were in my throat, and the only words that came out were "okay, now, how do we fix this?"

The therapist said, "Did you hear what I just said? There is *no* cure for autism. It's just that simple."

To which I responded, "I'm not buying that, and I'm going to help my son no matter what it takes. He will not be institutionalized unless my God says so. And He's not throwing in the towel on this kid. You have no idea what I've been through to get him in my life. Sorry! I'm not buying it."

As I was ready to leave in a state that words cannot begin to describe, she wrote down some referral phone numbers of people to contact to get Devin the best help available. She told me that early intervention was the key and apologized for being so blunt with the facts. I could not speak. I just took the piece of paper and left.

Given the strained relationship with my husband, how would I explain this? He was already in denial. This news would totally devastate our marriage. Where would I begin? How would I explain something that I did not understand myself?

Another life lesson was coming my way, and I was definitely not prepared for it. I thought, "Okay, God... I told You I was all in, but now I need some help. And I need a lot of it right away." From my perspective, the timing was all wrong. The Lord's timing, however, is always perfect.

God had to take His time with me. The challenge was not just with my husband. If I trusted His promises with all my heart, God could then mold my character in a fashion that could be recognized by others. This was not because I needed to be dealt with harshly. It was so that He might use me for His purposes and His glory.

At this point in my life, I did not fully understand what was happening or why. I had always tried to fight my battles in my own strength. I was about to discover just how little I could actually accomplish on my own. This battle I was about to face could not be won without God.

It was only a few months before my husband would be leaving for the winter to ride at a racetrack far from home. I was crying when I told him the news, but I did not get an ounce of sympathy. He said, "Do what you want. You never listen to me anyway, and I have no answers for you." Even my mother was in disbelief. I felt alone, confused, and without guidance.

I called the school board and therapy clinics to which I had been referred. It just so happened that I had only two weeks left before the schools would stop their evaluations for the upcoming school year. Once again, God's timing proved to be perfect. Although I felt I had no other support besides Him, I learned not to let the outside world control my emotions. That may not have been in the Lord's plan, but it worked for me.

The school board agreed with the initial diagnosis. They even helped to get Devin the early intervention he needed, and we got it as quickly as possible. I was given more people to contact, including government agencies that could be of assistance. Every person I approached pointed me in a direction that resulted in more help for Devin. This was now starting to take on substance. I knew we were looking at a long-term goal, so I started taking good care of myself physically and mentally. This boy would have as normal a life as possible, and I would be there to help him climb over every mountain he faced.

But, once again, I was reminded never to lower my guard. The enemy was always lurking around the corner of every success for which I gave God the glory. He knew each of my plans and all of my weaknesses. I always had to stay alert... especially when I thought things were going well.

Just as I thought I was laying the correct foundation for Devin's immediate future, the enemy used our marital discord in an attempt to break me.

3

BREAKING DOWN TO MY KNEES

"Our bodies are buried in brokenness, but they will be raised in glory. They are buried in weakness, but they will be raised in strength."

—1 CORINTHIANS 15:43

The Holidays were upon us, and my husband would be leaving soon for New Orleans. The winter horseracing season would begin on Thanksgiving Day, and things appeared to be going relatively well. Due to the autism, Devin started pre-school that year at a younger age than is normal. He would attend three days a week until his birthday in December, and that worked out fine.

I dreaded having to bring him to school because he had such terrible separation anxiety. Convinced, however, that being separated was something he needed, I was all the more persuaded that I needed it as well.

I had a house to take care of—washing, grocery shopping, and cooking—and all the typical daily requirements of being a mother, wife, and personal business assistant to my husband. We only sent him to school for half of each day, but it would take almost the entire time before he achieved some measure of peace. Would each day consist of such erratic behavior?

Considering his young age, the school made exceptions for his outbursts. In time, however, I feared they might not be so tolerant. If Devin had any chance to survive in this world, I was convinced he needed to learn how to adapt to life's many expectations and standards. Many days, however, it was I who could not help but cry the entire time he was gone. I was as much bound to him as he was to me.

There are always kids that make fun of the ones who are different. The names they called him actually hurt me more than they did Devin. Autism put him in his own little world, shutting out all the ugly that I saw. I suppose God had already equipped his young life with such personal defense mechanisms. My husband, in comparing Devin with other children, was beginning to see how different he was. In his own beautiful way, he was still quite special to us. It was through this daily battle that my husband's heart would also break as deeply as mine. Only, he was much better at masking those feelings than I.

My husband embarked very quietly on his journey to New Orleans. We were to join him later. We made our visit during the Thanksgiving holidays, which was the week off from school. This would start out with a very lengthy drive. Trying to manage the exceptionalities of a special child throughout the trip made our traveling much longer than ever before. I packed extra toys, videos, and snacks to make as few stops as possible. It was as if my body only knew one speed: GO. I was always on full throttle.

After we settled in, opening day on Thanksgiving gave us such joy to see our friends and family again. It was bittersweet without my father, but we pushed on.

The day that followed would be another day that would change our lives once again. That day, "Black Friday" was given a whole new meaning in my world. From that day forward, I began a walk through one of my darkest valleys yet.

On the last race of the day, my husband's horse got spooked and reared into the air. As she lost her footing, she fell back on top of him. A thousand-pound animal was in panic, kicking into the air, while lying on his frail, 112-pound body.

Although jockeys wear protective vests, they cannot sustain that kind of crushing power. It appeared, in my eyes, that everything was happening in slow motion. He was put on a gurney and rushed to the nearest trauma center as quickly as possible. I flung Devin in my arms and raced to the ambulance, telling him that I would be following right behind. As pain pulsated through his small body, all he could say was, "I'm so sorry, Honey. This one's bad… really bad."

Devin was clueless when it came to emotions. He could neither read them on another's face nor express how he felt about anything. The noise of the siren terrified him even more than the possible outcome of this accident terrified me. My life was about to become as uncomfortable as my son felt in this world.

My head was racing in every direction in the emergency room. I had no idea who I should call first. I didn't know what I was going to feed Devin, nor did I even have any diapers to change him. I had no clue how long I would be there. The fear of the unknown was starting to wash over me like a bad storm beginning to brew.

After what felt like a very long time, I was finally approached by three doctors who asked me to step out into the hallway. This had never happened before in all the injuries we had dealt with. One doctor was an orthopedic surgeon, one an internal medical surgeon, and the other was the emergency doctor on call. They told me that my husband was in ICU and that his injuries were multiple. Aside from seven broken ribs, he had a broken pelvis (in three places), lacerated liver, torn spleen, punctured bladder, and internal bleeding. I was asked to sign paperwork as quickly as possible to allow them to give him more blood and give him the care that was required.

Things were now becoming cloudy in my head, and I lost all sense of space and time. I just followed their instruction on what to do and where to go. I had no idea that this was day one in ICU of what would result in nearly a one-month stay. All I knew at this time was that he was in critical condition, requiring multiple surgeries, and that nothing could be fixed until they could get the bleeding to subside. There was a possibility that the liver would start to heal itself, but the other problems would require surgery. I had to stay there as such life-threatening injuries could cause something to change for the worse in an instant.

This hospital was in a bad part of town, and with New Orleans still recovering from Hurricane Katrina's havoc, everything was under construction. Devin and I got some crackers and bottled water from a vending machine. I made a call to a friend to bring a pack of diapers to me as Devin was still not able to use the bathroom on his own.

I was scared, alone, and now becoming quite exhausted. I pulled two chairs together to create a makeshift bed for both of us. I used my purse as a pillow and cradled Devin between my legs with both arms clenching him tightly. I was frightened by the thought of someone possibly snatching him from me while dosing off to sleep. I could only think of the worst that could happen now. I cried out to God for help, but I had no idea what to ask of Him. I thought that I was right with my Lord, but I had no idea what a personal relationship with Him was like… yet.

The night passed, and as morning broke through the window, a young intern greeted me with news that the internal bleeding was beginning to stop. The liver had also progressed in healing itself.

Another night went by, and I had only left the hospital to get food and a change of clothes for the two of us. Everything was hurting me, and I felt broken beyond repair. I cried out on that second night to Jesus. I awoke at 3:00 a.m. During more uncontrollable crying, I poured out my entire being to Him. I surrendered to my Lord and Savior. I admitted that this was way too big for me to deal with and that I was done, spent, empty, and did not want to face this battle anymore. As tears streamed from my eyes, I soon felt a calmness come over my entire body. I felt the power of the Holy Spirit cover me as never before. When I got to the point where the tears had begun drying, things started happening miraculously around me.

After that morning encounter, doctors began approaching me from out of the blue with news and results that would literally take my breath away. He was transported to another hospital for surgery to the pelvis and bladder. After the liver sealed itself, the spleen followed as well. Spleens do not typically heal themselves; however, his did. As I signed more paperwork to proceed with the other surgeries, I continued to speak to my Jesus on a moment-by-moment basis. It had become more than just daily now. It was as if He was sitting right beside me… never allowing me to feel alone again.

I was able to return to our trailer for the evenings as this new hospital would not allow me to bring Devin to the waiting room area of that floor. Things were still critical, but I was now allowing God to take over everything. Friends would appear from out of the blue to assist in watching Devin for me. Bonds were forming with total strangers and in the most uncanny of ways. I was beginning to experience what it was like to surrender totally to Christ.

As my life was being turned completely upside down (without any idea of what the next day might hold), I was walking in blind faith. When surgery was taking place on my husband's pelvis and bladder, I reached out to a woman who looked as broken as myself. Her daughter came in the same day from a car accident that was trying to take her life. I hugged her tightly and prayed over her. I had never done that before to anyone. It was as if it jumped right out of me automatically. We cried together, smiled, and believed that our Lord would do miracles in our lives. I shared my story with her and gave her hope that we were not alone.

You see, this is where His Word takes on new life... when two or more stand in agreement on God's promises. It was in sharing my testimony of His goodness and faithfulness that this hopeless situation turned into new possibilities.

It felt like the surgeons were taking an eternity to complete their work. A doctor stepped into the waiting room to call me out of the room. The first time this happened to me, news wasn't good. But this time, I was not the same person I had been before. I was expecting good results and standing firm on what my Heavenly Father was capable of. He was not going to let His little girl down, and He proved again His unwavering love for me.

The doctor said that the pelvis surgery went very well but that it would take time to see if his body would accept the hardware they used to reconstruct it. He also said that, surprisingly, the internal surgeons could not find the puncture wound in his bladder. The orthopedic surgeon said that, as puzzling as this seemed, he stayed in the room to ensure the accuracy of their findings. My husband's bladder was filled to maximum capacity three or four times. Each time, it never leaked a bit. The end result was that no bladder surgery was required. I smiled and told him that it was good he stayed to watch. That is how miracles are witnessed. He still looked puzzled as I just gave him the biggest hug and thanked him. I assured him that he would believe in time.

Although the surgery was a success, days would still go by like a teeter-totter. As one complication would develop, another would bring a miraculous result. Our Thanksgiving week turned into a roller coaster of twists and turns that kept us fully relying on God non-stop for a full month.

Devin and my husband had to be apart during that entire time because of the hospital rules and complexity of his injuries. But when he was finally released and sent by ambulance back to our home, everything started making more sense in our lives. Our plans and purpose were now put in God's hands to live the life He had called us to live. And He was faithful to deliver in spectacular ways.

We had no idea if my husband would be able to return to riding again. He would be non-weight bearing for another six months before seeing the outcome of the one and only surgery required. God had already fixed the remainder of the life-threatening issues at hand. Why should we begin doubting His amazing grace now? I became sold out to Jesus in an ICU room, and there was no turning away from Him anymore.

Once back home, it felt like we had a fresh outlook on life again. Although Devin's autism would still be there to deal with, he returned back to school as soon as possible. The enemy was not happy with my newfound freedom in Christ. Our son's separation anxiety returned, but I was blessed with wonderful people who would assist in the progress to follow. Devin's issues with loud noises continued as did his fear of domestic animals. At times, every step forward seemed to be followed by two steps backward. As a team, I worked diligently with the teachers and therapists for my son.

Although things appeared quite difficult, I was ready to take on the challenges with God now. But saying that and living that are two different things. I realized that, if I was to believe in miracles, I had to speak them into reality. I had to trust blindly without my own reasoning. I had to share the testimony of His goodness with others and also dive into God's Word for the wisdom that He wanted me to acquire. When I began to do these things, change started taking place within me. Joy flowed into my heart, and hope was the anchor that kept me grounded.

My husband's recovery period lasted almost a year. During that time, as he was becoming stronger physically (to return to riding), he was also growing stronger spiritually. We prayed as a team for miracles to occur in Devin. We attended the local church regularly as well. Chaplains and pastors stood in agreement with us for total healing of our son's condition. As Devin would sit in church, either coloring or napping to remain quietly occupied, Jesus began working in his life as well.

Autism is like a mask that hides the inside of an individual's soul. Though, it can never beat God. He carefully created each of us so beautifully in His eyes. It is up to us to reveal that beauty to the rest of the world.

God blessed us with healing in my husband so that he could return to work and continue providing for us. During the time of his recovery, our Lord handled all matters regarding our cost of living. Unexpected things happened that helped us to remain financially stable. Aside from having savings put away for emergencies, people from all over the world helped us as well. When bills came in the mail, there would always be something coming in to cover them.

Only a loving and caring eternal Father can answer needs in such a manner. Trusting in *Him* will unlock many doors.

Once returning back to a somewhat normal life for my husband and me, Devin's progress was still creeping at a slow pace. We believed so passionately and had been blessed so much that we thought he would be receiving an equal portion as well. It seemed like my son was trapped in this ongoing, daily struggle with fear and solitude.

I broke down one night when autism had been getting the best of me. I cried out to God, once again, to heal my son, fix this problem, and make him normal. But in that hour, I was awakened to something very unexpectedly. I felt the Lord speak to my heart in a way I had never heard before. He told me firmly but lovingly,

> I created Devin perfectly in My eyes. It is you who needs to learn more than him. He is untainted by this world and sees things simply and beautifully... as I intended. His world is pure, and understands no evil. The noises that bother his tender ears are from things made by man... not *by me*. Learn from him, yet teach him My Word. And know, My Child, I am always with you.

I don't think I ever cried so hard in all the trials I faced. It was me who needed to be fixed... not my son. God had a plan for his life, and even though he was mine, Devin was always His first. I realized that I was only allowed to have him on this earth for a short time in comparison to eternity. It was my job to show him how God works in our lives. In the right timing, he would come to understand God's goodness, righteousness, and deep love for all of us. I needed to plant His Holy Word in Devin for it to sprout and grow with strong roots. And through this personal encounter with the Most High, I was given direction in my walk with God.

Our track chaplain and one of my dearest friends gave me the help I needed to carry out God's orders. He soon became my mentor and teacher, instructing me spiritually with Bible verses for healing, restoration, peace, and guarding oneself from the enemy's attacks. He explained to me how important and powerful the Word of God actually is. He told me that speaking these words over Devin, myself, or anyone else was how we could access His power to bring things into existence. This was how I was introduced to the Holy Spirit, who is my Comforter, Counselor, and Almighty Intercessor.

As I became more knowledgeable about the Scriptures, I felt the need to express my gratitude to Jesus for all that He had done for me. I wanted to do something that showed I was all His. And when I asked our chaplain about baptism, he was more than happy to do the honors. I had already been baptized as a baby as part of my Catholic religion—as were Devin and my husband—but I read how Jesus was baptized as an adult before He started His ministry. I thought, "Lord, if that was what You did, so will I." Now, whether it mattered or not to have it done more than once was not important to me. I made this decision because I was committing—or recommitting—my life to Him. It was strictly an act between my Savior and me. My life had changed, and I was ready to give Him what was left of it for His work. No longer did I feel that I was living for myself, for I was now living for Him. And I continued to see more things happen with every step I made along my journey with God.

4

STANDING FIRMLY ON HIS WORD

"The Word gave life to everything that was created, and His life brought light to everyone."

—JOHN 1:4

It was now time to get started on my spiritual plan of action for Devin's life. I told the Lord that I no longer would expect to see results according to my timing but according to His. I needed to learn how to develop the fruits of the Spirit in my own life as I would try to set a good example for my son to follow as he grew. Patience and self-control would be my most difficult to attain.

I had already been down the road of different diets for my son with no success. Speech and occupational therapy were still a part of our lives, but I trusted that God would be the One to direct the course of these different methods. The more I prayed, the more special people crossed our paths. And with each encounter, I noticed that Devin was changing their lives as well. It did not matter how qualified someone was. Their interaction with him taught them things about themselves, the Lord, and faith in the possibilities of the unknown. He brought out the purity in each person who took the time to be involved in his life. My conversations with God gave me more wisdom and put me on the path of His direction. How could I go wrong?

Because the internet was the main place where we all went for more information, I began looking for easy access to the Bible verses I needed for healing. Once I found that, the search was on. Healing, deliverance, faith, and spiritual power were among the many things I searched for. I discovered verses that were beyond informative. God's Word from thousands of years ago still provided the accurate instruction I needed to apply to our situation today. I copied three to four pages of healing scriptures alone from my online Bible to print. These, in particular, were spoken over my son every night as part of our prayer ritual. I declared that, not only would I learn these by heart, Devin would also learn these as well. My son said very few words as I started this plan. His interaction with others was at a minimum. You could ask him simple questions and, if you got eye contact, it was progress. I longed for the day when I would hear, "I love you, Mom", more than anyone could imagine.

He still continued lining up toys, walking on his toes, and pressing his chin into hard surfaces as a self-soothing technique. He went crazy with loud noises, and trying to get him to wear headphones to help suppress these sounds was impossible. He would tolerate nothing on his head and no tags on his clothes. Interaction with other children was unheard of. Also, the idea of taking a walk down the street was not even fathomed. If he saw a dog or cat (as much as a block away), fear would drive him into a frenzy. He would be scaling your back like a thief over a fence in a matter of seconds just to increase his distance from them. We never experienced the "terrible twos" phase in Devin's life. His fears kept him by my side at all times possible.

But during the times when he felt secure enough to drift away from me, it was I who had to panic. Things he should never have attempted would draw his attention like a magnet. We visited a park one day that housed wild cats of all species. All of these cats had been abused. Devin would walk up to the fence and try his hardest to reach in and touch them. A kitten would petrify him, but a 600-pound lion gave him the urge to cuddle up to and show affection. Around horses, I would always have to pay close attention to ensure that he did not run behind or underneath one. His amazement of cars was even worse. He could easily dart in front of a moving car without any hesitation concerning the probable outcome. The vast array of these types of things that occurred in my world daily were not even imagined by a typical outsider. And to put my trust in God was literally my only resort. Without believing that my situation would improve, I would have remained hopeless.

At school, Devin was learning to communicate through a system called PACS, which stands for "Picture Archiving and Communication System." Devin had his own special PACS book to work on. The wonderful Pre-K teacher who we were blessed to have started him out with this tool. The goal was that he would reach higher levels of focus, as well as necessary communication skills. I was delighted that he had something to work with, but that was not helping our communication at home. I told her that I would buy the same package they were using if she could meet with me and show me how to use these tools. She was a very caring woman, so she took the time to make a few sets of laminated cards for me to use at home. It was a huge start for me. I was now learning what Devin was learning, and this was the turning point for us as I was now able to collaborate with his teachers more effectively.

We became close as family through each grade he moved into. We all worked together through each of his obstacles toward achieving the same goals. This unity continues even today as we take the time and initiative to treat the people in our lives with dignity and respect. There were IEP evaluations (Individual Education Plans) each year. They were intended to keep a chart of the goals we had decided on as a team to try to acquire throughout the year. I had heard many horror stories from other parents who had a difficult time at these meetings. Some of them resulted in huge arguments with faculty and staff, and some went as far as having to change schools. But in my case, very few disagreements took place. We all left our meetings smiling and with ideas shared at the table to try out at home as well as at school.

I was involved in Devin's life as much as I could be. Activities, field trips, and working with teachers were pieces forming the center of our devotion and hope in God's plan. At the end of each day, when tucking him into bed at night, we prayed to our Lord. As the words came from my mouth,

Devin's attention was focused on me. I prayed the prayers of healing over him and repeatedly made the sign of the cross on his forehead. At the time, I did not know that these prayers were being absorbed into his mind and spirit each night. I was planting seeds that would later begin to bloom in the most beautiful ways I had ever expected. But that's exactly how God works in each of us. He touches those with a child-like nature in remarkable ways. His miracles are not ordinary but spectacular in their complexity and originality. Our Heavenly Father takes the impossible things of this world and uses the most unlikely things to turn them completely around in the other direction. And with each new thing He revealed to me, I fell deeper in love with Him.

At the end of kindergarten, Devin was now going to the bathroom on his own. Wiping himself was still a challenge, but the diapers and pull-ups were a thing of our past. His name was coming up on some of the government programs he was enlisted for. But we put each new milestone in God's hands. This did not make me a patient parent at all, but I was getting there, step by step. I read the Bible daily as did my husband. We shared different things we were finding in the Word that pertained to our situation. It was revealing truths that we had not been aware of before. But still, when we went to school functions, we continued to feel completely out of place.

Other kids were talking more and interacting with each other, but our son was on his own and constantly had to be roped into a group activity. We heard children talking about how he was strange. They never wanted to play with him and just looked at him funny most of the time. Our hearts broke regularly with each encounter. Watching the rest of them play—except in the special education class—made me wonder what our future really held.

The enemy slips into our minds when we allow him that freedom and feeds on our emotions ravenously. I tried convincing myself that, if Devin were to grow up voicing his own opinion, he may just get himself into trouble. Too much mischief could get him involved with the wrong type of friends, and I certainly did not want that path for him. So through this twisted roller coaster of emotions, I decided to just pack the heartbreak away and give my tears to God.

At church, I always packed notebooks and colors for Devin to draw in. This would keep him quiet throughout the service without disturbing the adults. Coloring, as children normally do, was not the same in our house. Devin drew his own pictures and ignored the figures in all coloring books. He even wrote words by his pictures as well. This was when we discovered that he could spell more than talk. Although he was learning to say a few words, his sentences did not make any sense. Not even short sentences were used… only a few words and pointing. But when he had a pen in his hand, he would write words like *hippopotamus, crocodile, Antarctica*, and many others just as difficult.

He was addicted to his portable DVD player and loved watching the documentaries about nature and various wild animals. Little did I know that, as he watched these movies, he was memorizing everything. And when I say *everything*, that is exactly what I mean. He knew all of the directors' names, actors, writers, and any credits, dates, or places in which a movie was filmed. His memory was phenomenal. His vision and hearing were also incredible as well. He could spot a truck down the road and tell you what was written on the side of it or a telephone number that flashed across the television… weeks later. His hearing was so precise that, if a neighbor three houses away was cutting grass, Devin covered his ears and screamed.

It took a long time to discover what was wrong with him until we finally realized how acute his senses were. Blowers and weed eaters were the worst. Their sounds were so deafening to his ears that I would have to get in the car and drive him somewhere. I begged the people around us to do their yardwork on a weekday while he was at school. The lawn equipment had become such a big issue, in fact, that it affected his performance in school. The teachers would inform me of his behavior when they cut the school grass. And luckily, they would make allowances for him during those times. There was an endless list of things in our lives that were strange and unusual, but we muddled through each one, continuing to lean on God.

Among the other odd things that were normal routines in our lives, we also had problems when Devin was sick. Trips to the doctor and dentist were some of my worst nightmares brought into reality. After he got his first set of shots and blood drawn from his finger, we realized that his memory of events became *our* biggest fear. The drive there started with crying from the moment I got off the exit. And getting Devin through the door of the doctor's office required help from two or more people. He literally had to be carried in, holding his arms and legs together, in order to pass through the doors. I wondered what would happen as he grew more or if something took place requiring a hospital stay. These thoughts made me as overwhelmed as my son. I felt as autistic as he during these times.

But then, in the midst of a "normal" day in our house, Devin wrote a part of one of the songs we sang in church on a piece of paper and handed it to me. I was blown away. I ran to my husband and shared it with him. He wrote the lyrics, "I'm trading my sorrows. I'm trading my shame. I'm laying them down for the joy of the Lord." This was from a song we sang in church but not on a regular basis. We knew now that God was moving in a powerful way! All of those trips to church with colors and a sketch book were masking what was being planted on the inside. He was getting it. In his odd, preoccupied mind, our son was getting the message of God's Word. The Holy Spirit was interpreting to him in his own language so that he could understand. This, in itself, was a full-blown miracle, and many more were about to occur.

I continued to pray to God for more wisdom and direction. I was already testifying to others of His wonderful miracles and favor that were being poured out upon us. With the Word of God now moving in Devin's life, I had to help him work around his deepest fears. It was imperative that we establish some sort of communication between us. I needed Devin to express himself better so that I would know how he felt about things. Being more aware of the times when he was scared could help me avoid a full-blown drama. I had to know when sickness was upon him before a fever jumped to 104. He needed to be able to express all of these different emotions in a calmer manner, using words that we could all understand. During the times when his emotions were heightened, gibberish flew out of his mouth. And the speech that he already had learned was thrown into an abyss while those emotions elevated.

One morning, I awoke to a message that God had placed on my heart. It was as simply put as, "I will make things possible through the impossible." As my day progressed, I wondered just what impossible things the Lord was working on. I got so excited with this message that my impatience had me trying to discover new things on my own. That only resulted in little success. You see, when the Almighty has a plan to work out things in your life, you need to just step aside and allow *Him* to do the work. He does not need your help with His plan unless He gives you instructions to follow. And so, I waited for a sign. This was also part of my Lord's strategy to develop patience and trust in my character. He had been molding me all along as He was guiding me to parent my son. During these times when we wait on God, thinking that He is doing nothing, things are already being put into action. As the world moves quickly around us, we can lose sight of its beauty in an instant. And sometimes, while you are trusting Him for help, God forces us to stop and behold what is right in front of our very eyes.

As I was running some errands with Devin on a Saturday morning, I was caught up in traffic, which was testing my nerves. A man on the side of the road was holding up a PET ADOPTION DAY sign at the local pet store in the strip mall. I thought to myself, *Yeah right… As if that will ever happen to us.* And in that very moment, I felt a tug on my heart. Something was stirring inside of me, and I had no idea what it was. I pulled into the shopping center, and as I got closer to the pet store parking lot, people were walking out with dogs and cats of all sorts. Devin was in the car and actually remained calm as he looked through the window at them. I said, "Honey, do you want to go inside and see the animals in there?"

Abruptly, he said, "No."

So, I parked the car at a short distance away as we watched these people and animals from the windows. A quiet reaction from Devin—in this setting—was a small step forward. I was quite pleased that he was remaining so tranquil. This was step one on our road to one accomplishment. I now knew what God meant by the impossible. And I trusted Him, taking the time each week to do a little more than the week before.

It became a regular routine to go to the pet store. We visited during the week to look at the fish and reptiles in the tanks as well as the birds in their cages. Devin was good with this as long as he did not touch their glass containers. On Saturdays, when they brought in the dogs and cats from homeless shelters, we went. At first, we stayed in the car near the doors. But, each week, we would get a bit closer... just inside, peering from an aisle at a distance or walking near a cage without touching it. Then, finally, he accidently bumped into a dog that they were bringing back into its crate. With that incident, he threw a bit of a fit, and it was time to leave. But one of the helpers there noticed us each week and knew that Devin was struggling with this fear. He came and talked to me outside and spoke to Devin without receiving a response. He told him his name and that he would be there next week with a special puppy that he could touch if he wanted to. Again, Devin did not respond (as usual), and I thanked the young man for trying.

The following week would be different. Devin remembered the conversation and insisted, "Puppy, Momma.

Puppy." So, off we went, not knowing what to expect. We arrived before the animals got there, and a quiet store was always a good beginning. Then, the parade of pets came in. They were so noisy, and Devin held his ears tightly, pacing back and forth on the farthest aisle from the cages. He spotted the young man who he now considered his friend. When things quieted, Devin went to him and tugged on his shirt softly. As he turned around, smiling at him, he remembered the puppy promise. He brought Devin, who was clinging tightly to my hand, over to a cage with a brown, mixed-breed that was a bit large. Devin refused to allow the boy to take him out of the cage, but he did stick his finger in to touch the dog's hair. This was step two in achieving our goal of the impossible. This was enough for him for one day, and that was alright with me. We were making baby steps forward, and fear of man's best friend was slowly diminishing.

I went home so excited that not only I but Devin as well was spilling out the adventure to my husband in words that made no sense. I was sounding as uncomprehending as my son, and we were both dancing around the house like it was the happiest day of our lives. My husband said, "Tell me you did not buy a dog!"

I said, "Of course not. But… I think God has other plans further down the line."

He knew we were not able to take on the responsibility that came with owning a dog. Devin still had a long way to go before we actually thought this interaction would work on a daily basis, but I was basking in the possibilities that the Lord was showing me. I was embracing the fact that He could make anything happen out of nothing. And, as my trust in Him grew, so did the progress. We continued our visits until we got to the point where Devin would actually hold a puppy and even kiss one on the head. But still, we had a long way to go before owning one. Daily interactions with a dog require more time and practice.

We visited some local dog shows, which were more difficult than I imagined. I failed to consider all the noise from the blow dryers that were used to primp them up for the events. We met a few people there who gave us sound advice on the right choice of dog to consider for Devin. There were many who thought this was a crazy idea… except for one. She was a judge who not only observed the dogs in the ring but Devin's behavior around them as well. She asked, "Your boy has autism? He needs a dog that's calmer than he is, or they'll both make you crazy." And she was right. She had an old Field Spaniel back at her house and insisted that this was the breed for him. When I began my search for this breed, it was nearly impossible to find one. They are one of the rarest of dogs in the world. The nearest breeder that I could find through an internet search was in Texas and had no puppies for sale. She bred two females and did not know if either was pregnant yet. We then had to put our name on a list below 50 others in hopes that she might have the answer to our prayers. Well, let me just say that, when God is moving and shifting events for you, *all* things are possible.

The waiting process in this adventure brought new friends into our lives who would witness to miracles and God's power through faith and prayer. They would touch our lives in ways that mere words never could. My husband thought I had lost my mind in all of this until he saw how things unfolded. Only three puppies were born from the first female, and at the end of a line of 50, things did not

WALKING WITH GOD THROUGH AUTISM

"look" hopeful. But, in times when our Lord moves moun-
tains, He also brings change to peoples' hearts.

As I became closer to this breeder during our wait and
many conversations, a bond was formed. Devin saw the pictures of the puppies, and surprisingly, without seeing them
physically, he already had one picked out and a name as
well. He was making decisions now. This alone was something we had not expected in our wildest of fantasies. The
breeder was so moved by our faith in God that she allowed
Devin to get the puppy he wanted. She said that it brought
her joy to be part of such a wonderful thing.

But when the day came to pick up our little girl and
bring her home, Devin was frightened. We had a crate in the
back of the car, and she whined all the way home during
our long drive. I asked, "God, is this part of the plan, too?"
But as my son saw how scared she was, he started feeling
sorry for her. I explained to him that she was missing her
mom and the other pups. By now, we were both telling her
it was going to be okay and that she would love her new
home with us. She was a part of our abnormal family now
and would always be loved.

Once home, she was as bashful at warming up to Devin
as he was to her. He slowly touched her through the crate,
little by little. Then, as the day went on, he started brushing
her. He even kissed her head goodnight. The dog judge was
right all along. This was the perfect breed of dog for him.
She never jumped on him, licked his face persistently, or got
hyper at all. They were made for each other and appeared
to be cut from the same cloth. God knew exactly what He
was doing all along. He made something possible in the
middle of the impossible. He allowed my son to have his

closest relationship—outside of ours—with an animal that terrified him the most. Now, that's an amazing God!

He named her Rosebud for whatever reason he had, and she blossomed into the most beautiful of roses. She became a loyal companion to each of us in her own special way. Within that first year, Devin would come home from school and lay his head on her side. He would pull out a book and begin reading to her in very short, simple sentences. She would look at his every move and observe him as if he was her own personal responsibility. She would sit in the bathroom while I gave him a bath and lick the water off the back of his neck and shoulders. When he was sick, she never left his side and would alarm me when his fever would get high. Her unique gifts earned her the SERVICE DOG OF THE YEAR title in no time.

And not only had our Rosebud been a personal gift from God to our son, she was there for our needs as well. It was also within this year of growth and change that I heard the phrase my heart so longed to hear: "I love you, Mom." These words were spoken from my son's mouth with no prompting him to repeat the words from someone else. Faith was bringing our family to a high that started turning heads. People were now taking notice of Devin's incredible progress.

But the enemy hates to see anyone reap from the rewards of believing in Jesus Christ. He is ready to bring chaos in the midst of your rejoicing.

When the future is unknown, our Heavenly Father has a path planned out for us that becomes more visible as time goes on. Always trusting Him must become the backbone in each of our lives. Our bodies have been uniquely woven together by our Divine Creator, cell by cell. But we are also knit with one another in relationships that we cannot begin to understand. There are always crossroads and turning points that we each face where our decisions direct those paths. It is up to us as to whether we will choose to follow our own or God's.

As I continue in describing my spiritual journey, I hope that it will bring some clarity to your own path in life. I had to realize how incredibly huge God's love was for me before I could continue trusting Him in the unknown. Sometimes, that trust has to be declared over ourselves daily. It is necessary to carry on no matter what you have to go through. And when He reveals His wonders, we can hold to them as proof that He will never let us down. He goes before us, follows us, and will even carry us through the darkest and deepest valleys we face. With each challenge I walked through, my endurance increased. And as that endurance developed, my character became stronger, bringing hope and faith to a more meaningful place.

5

SUITING UP FOR BATTLE

*"Put on all of God's armor so that you will be able
to stand firm against all strategies of the devil."*

—EPHESIANS 6:11

God's Word tells us to expect problems and trials, so why is it such a surprise when they fall upon us? The bad situations that occur do not always result from our choices. If this were the case, wouldn't we *all* choose to live without sickness and sorrow? And when unexpected news devastates our world, is it not then that we quickly try mustering survival plans of our own? Sometimes, things happen that overwhelm and shatter one's entire being. And in the events that followed on my journey, they did just that. I was forced to go to the next level in my faith. It was essential that I trust God more blindly than ever before.

After my husband remarkably returned back to the racing world—with a fire for Christ burning brighter within him than ever before—other things started to occur. He just was not quite right. His business was slowly faltering, and he would get wearier in doing things we normally did. When he was home, he never wanted to leave the house unless it was for racing or church. We discussed the idea of retiring soon, but—as with all athletes—this is a subject most tender to address. When I questioned him regarding future plans, he never had a response. His demeanor appeared to be always tuning me out or possibly just evading an answer. I knew this was a very difficult decision to make. Especially for a person who had performed in the public eye for four decades. It's not easy to separate the man you are from the man you're going to become. Change is hard for all of us. But we were slowly becoming caught in a whirlwind that took us in a completely different direction.

The winter meet was about to end in another two months down south. I received a phone call from my husband out of the blue, declaring that he was going to become a jockey agent. He told me that he had already announced his retirement to the track and even to the press earlier that morning. I was shocked not about the news but about the way he suddenly announced it. He had just reacted without even telling me anything. He said he was tired and was packing everything to head back home. He would start out in May when the track near our house would open.

I was somewhat hurt that he didn't call me first about this decision. The world knew our plans before I did. This was not like him at all. We had not been arguing and always talked about things of the slightest importance. Something just did not add up. When your gut feeling tells you that something is out of sorts, you learn to trust it. This is how the Holy Spirit urges you to hear His voice.

Later that night as my husband returned home and came through the door, our dog went wild with barking. She acted as if he were a stranger breaking in. I kept telling her that it was "Daddy." How could a dog not know her own master? When she finally heard his voice and smelled him, she was acting sorry for her reaction by cuddling up to him as much as possible. He looked horrible. He was skinny and limping like an old man that I did not know. I told him to just go lay down for a bit after the long drive and that I would unpack his truck myself.

When I got outside to the truck, everything had been thrown in the back as if balled up in a huge knot. Nothing was secured, and God only knew the things that had flown out during that six-hour drive home.

As I walked back inside with an armful of things, I saw him lying on the floor in our bedroom. I dropped the things and ran to him. "What happened, Honey? Did Devin or the dog knock you down? Are you okay?"

He was out of breath somewhat and said that Devin had just come in to give him a hug. But this was not right at all. I told him to let me take him to the hospital or call 911 if he could not get up. This made him grow angrier than I'd ever seen him get. He said, "No way! I'm fine! Don't you dare pick up that phone!" He said he was just tired from the drive and from packing. As his tone got calmer, I convinced myself to believe him over my own instincts. I just wanted everything to be alright, but there remained a pulling inside of me that would not let up. I finished unpacking the truck and helped him get into bed to rest. Tomorrow would be a new day… but not a better one.

After Devin and he fell asleep, I began to pray. I knelt down by the side of my bed and poured my heart out to God. I didn't know what was happening, but all of this had me so anguished and unsettled. I needed Him to guide me and tell me what was going on. What was I supposed to do? Just ignore all that took place before my eyes? As I received no answer, my tears made me tired enough to attempt falling asleep.

But then, as I laid in bed with my heart open to God's voice, an amazing thing happened. I had a vision of my Lord at the foot of my bed, down on one knee. He was holding a bowl and a towel. I could only see His back and thought, at first, that an angel had come to me. I had never experienced such a thing, but I will never forget it as the experience was embedded in my heart.

This supernatural being began to wash my feet. Only, this was not with water but with a warm, soothing love that was indescribable. I knew in my soul that it was Jesus. As I felt this incredible love start at my feet, it permeated my whole body… all the way through the hairs on my head.

As tears flowed down my face, I felt so unworthy of such an intense act of love. I whispered to Him, "Lord, why me? I know how much you love me, but what is happening? Why would You honor me with such an undeserving act? What is it that I have to walk through for You to wash my feet?" I felt His peace cover me in a nurturing blanket of protection, and I fell asleep immediately.

This can be doubted by the entire world as to what happened that night. But as the days unfolded, I was only reassured that my Lord would carry me through whatever we had to face.

The next morning, I got Devin off to school, and when I returned home, my husband had already gotten up. I smelled something burning in the house. Panic quickly fell upon me. He explained that it was from heating a cup of coffee too long in the microwave.

When I looked at the cup on the counter, I noticed that it was cracked with just powdered cream glued to the bottom. I asked, "Did you forget to add the coffee when you heated it?"

Then, he casually replied, "Yeah."

I also noticed he was using his left hand to lift and move his right hand. Not only were red flags waving, but his ankles and knees were extremely swollen as well. I told him that I was calling my regular doctor to see if he could slip him in that day to check things out. He agreed, and from that moment on, God's hand was steering our course.

We went in, and the doctor gave him some shots for the swelling and took blood to run tests. He thought perhaps the swelling was due to a case of gout. But then, as he looked at my husband more intently, something stirred the doctor's suspicion.

The doctor ordered x-rays to be taken of my husband's chest, and the results were not good. They showed a mass attached to his lung that was three-quarters the length of that lung. He ordered CT scans but was quite certain that this was an advanced stage of lung cancer. The road to treatment would be a long one. My mouth was wide open in shock because it had been more than three years since he had quit smoking. But my husband just sat there with a blank look on his face as if he had not heard a single word the doctor said. CT scans were taken immediately, and their results confirmed that the x-ray findings were accurate.

He was scheduled to see a pulmonary specialist the following day, which turned into complete chaos. Shortly after speaking to the surgeon, he insisted that my husband should be admitted into the hospital for a biopsy as soon as possible. Everything seemed to be happening so rapidly. I was screaming on the inside for the world to just stop. A nurse came in afterward to set up all the details, but I was fit to be tied. I could only hear her rambling about how much we would have to pay in advance that day. We did not have much money coming in before he retired, but now, there was nothing. Our health insurance was only affordable with a huge deductible. I explained that, if we had to pay the required amount up front, we would be down to almost nothing. I don't know how all of that came spewing from my mouth, but it did.

As she sat on the armrest of my chair, I felt her arms wrap tightly around me. My body went limp with weakness. She said, "Look, let me make a few phone calls and see what I can do. We are just going to hold off on admitting him for now." I sat in that office with my husband who was now a very different man than years before. He was not reacting to anything they said but remained sitting quietly as if in deep thought. When the nurse returned, she told us that LSU hospital would take him quickly because we had insurance. They could also work with us financially regarding our deductibles and other costs. She already had an appointment set with a specialist there for the next day. So we left and headed back home, just in time to get Devin from school. Our God was now behind the wheel driving, and we could do no more than accompany Him as mere passengers.

Devin loved on his daddy like it was a vacation. To have him home to hug and be in his presence was all he needed. I notified the school teachers of what we were going through, and they were extremely supportive throughout the entire rollercoaster we had been strapped into involuntarily.

When we arrived at the hospital, the new specialist took more x-rays, scans, and an MRI. This was done after discussing his strange behavior and the inability of his right limbs to work properly. He said that it might take a couple of days for the reports to come in and that he would call us with results.

The weather was starting to get bad, and we ran to the school to pick up our son together. My husband was in the worst of moods from being questioned and tested the entire day. As we picked up dinner, returning home as soon as possible, my cell phone was ringing from the doctor we had just left. He was calling personally to tell me to get my husband back to the hospital immediately. Things had become more serious than mere lung cancer. This monster had metastasized throughout his entire brain as well. He had to be hospitalized for a biopsy to identify what type of cancer it was now. They needed to determine whether brain surgery would have to be done quickly or not.

I think I was in borderline shock as a ball knotted up in my chest. I knew how angry he had been on the way home and clarified this to the doctor. I explained to him that my son had autism, and there was no one to watch him for us. The trauma of hospitals was still quite fresh in Devin's mind from the last hospital nightmare he had to endure. And to bring a very angry man back while dragging along our son would be extremely difficult. We had to come up with a better plan. How did these words even come from my mouth? It was as if I was a robot, and the things I was saying had been pre-recorded.

The doctor responded, "Do you understand what I'm telling you?"

I said, "Yes, I do. I understand quite clearly. But do you understand that, considering this bad weather and the state of mind I'm in, it could be detrimental to all of us if I leave now?"

He agreed but warned me, stressing the importance of my husband's condition, in case anything was to happen suddenly.

I said, "Here's the plan… We are going to bed early tonight. I will bring my son to school in the morning and go straight to the hospital with my husband. Then, we will do whatever needs to be done at the hospital tomorrow. How does that sound? What could happen at home that you can fix over there tonight?" Again, I was speaking in a most-unusual manner with plans flying completely out of the blue. This was definitely a God thing.

He replied, "Well, he could have a seizure, go into a coma during the night, or just not wake up at all. The choice is yours."

I said, "Then, I would call 9-1-1 and get an ambulance to get him to you as quickly as possible." At that, he hesitated for a bit and then agreed that it was a good plan of action. He did not have to say what he thought about his condition. I could already tell in his urgent tone what was happening. I just didn't quite fathom the reality of it all until the next morning. Perhaps I was just getting used to trusting in the Lord.

That night was one of the longest in my life. I could not sleep as the doctor's words were repeating in my head. I talked to my Savior the entire night... in bed and out. I was grateful that my husband was not having any pain. (At least, he never showed it.) I thanked God in advance for always being with me through each and every battle. I held on to His hand tightly and testified aloud that His grace was sufficient... even without knowing what would be the outcome.

When adversity looked me square in the face, I had two choices: deal with it or don't. It was how I dealt with my trials that defined me. Would I stand on a firm foundation, or allow the storm to flatten me to the ground? I built my foundation on God's promises... not those of this world. And sometimes, we have to blindly declare them over our situations. So, before the battle started, I got prepared with my best friend, Jesus.

Perhaps it was a good thing to be lacking in rest that day. After getting Devin and my husband ready, I calmly got my son to school and then quickly back to the hospital. As we checked into the emergency room, the doctors on-call were already awaiting our arrival. Usually, these visits test one's patience while waiting for one's name to be called. But that morning was very different than the others. We were directed in rather quickly as a young doctor pulled me aside with the brain scans. He was waiting for the specialist to arrive. He showed me a scan of a normal brain in comparison to my husband's, and the visual was enough to show the severity of his illness.

I started crying and had so many questions cluttering my mind, but no words would come out. He said, "Please, say something. Do you know how bad this looks?"

I said, "Yes, my father had Stage-4 lung cancer, and I think I'm looking at the same thing now. Am I right?"

He just nodded yes. He asked me who was going to break this news to my husband. And I said, "Well, you're the doctor, so you do it. I'll be there at his side to help him understand. But, please, give me a little time to digest this, and let me call my mother first. We have no family here to be with us right now." But that was not true because the Lord had been there the entire time. He knew what was going to take place long before I asked Him to come into my life.

That phone call to my mother was most difficult. She had spent time with my husband just days before he returned home. My mother also thought something had been peculiar in his recent behavior, but reality had not reached her mind either. I cannot remember what I said when I called her. It wasn't important how I said it but that she knew what we were dealing with. I asked her to tell the small remainder of our family, and then, I would tell my husband's family. Those phone calls were a blur. I depended on my family to spread this news for me. I didn't realize that the press would be calling for information as well. I would not answer their calls until we had confirmation of every doctor's opinion involved as well as the results from a biopsy.

He was immediately checked into the hospital on the top floor where the most serious cases were treated. It was quiet, and they prepped him for the biopsy the next day.

I went home that afternoon to get Devin from school. I prayed during the entire drive to the school, asking God to intervene even more than He had in the past. Devin was probably going to need the most help among us during this walk. I felt like I was the crutch for both of them to lean on. How would I get him to understand what was happening? How would I prepare him for his biggest loss… if God chose to take my husband home? Tears streamed endlessly from my eyes. And so, I strapped myself in tightly for this ride that already had begun.

The following day came and went. The biopsy results came back quickly. The cancer he had was a very fast-growing type, and it was taking over a small-framed man without any mercy. This Stage-4 demon was setting a timeframe on us that only God could control. He was given less than a year to live… which, in the doctors' minds, was only a few months. They determined that any treatment done would not be to save him but merely to help in making the remainder of his life a little better, and possibly, longer.

Chemotherapy was not an option as it would take him quicker and would have no effect on the cancer in his brain. Radiation teamed up with steroids would be used on his brain to decrease the size of the mass and try to reduce the swelling it was causing. This would only help for so long as the mass on his lung would be working against him. We talked about the treatments before leaving the hospital, and the doctors agreed that radiation therapy might help him somewhat. It could possibly allow him to use his right side more as well as with his speech. It was a plan. And so, we prayed each night for God's mercy and deliverance in this battle.

I had to tell our son this news in the best way I could, and that was much harder on me than it was for Devin. I picked up Devin from school on a day before treatments would start. I pulled the car into a nearby parking lot before getting back to the house. How I explained his father's illness was almost immediately forgotten. But regardless, it worked. I tried holding back the tears, yet they streamed uncontrollably. I remember asking him over and over, "Do you understand what Mom is telling you? Do you know that Dad is very sick again?"

His reply finally came out as he stared emotionlessly into my eyes. "I know, Mom. Dad... he's very sick." With hearing that, I just wiped my face, kissed him, and returned home.

I would have to confront the media and newspapers in the racing world soon. So, the Holy Spirit was now in charge of my words, and I gave Him control of all that came from my mouth.

Our friends and family members made every day a bit easier by their countless efforts to help us. Visits from those we loved were a reward for both us and for them. Prayers on our behalf had been sent throughout the country and even abroad. God's promises were already being seen in ways indescribable. To face each new day, I would prepare myself each morning in prayer, wearing the entire body armor of Christ. This was not easy. It was a daily struggle, but we were never alone.

The up-and-down moments throughout his treatments were constant. The side effects alone took their toll on us with repeated trips to the hospital. But when the radiation was finally over, the quality of our time together was awesome. My husband was not able to walk again, yet the memories shared remain unforgettable. Most importantly, our faith in the Lord had grown enormously, regardless of the outcome He planned. Our brothers and sisters in Christ took part in many gatherings at the house for praise, worship, and communion with us as well. And throughout each gathering, our Heavenly Father's presence came in a powerful way. All who entered our house felt a love and peace fall upon them that was unlike anything they had ever felt before.

As time passed, we became more aware of God's plan. Into the fourth month since the initial diagnosis, I knew in my heart that it was time to start preparing for the inevitable. We had wonderful talks together that were so personal and meaningful. Throughout our entire relationship, with all that we had shared, death would have to be part of our exquisite union.

I believe that he and God also had many conversations together. I believe that he was already prepared for the next chapter of his life. Being able to let go of us for that journey was his hardest thing to face.

One of the most memorable of things we discussed was a cross necklace that my husband always wore. It was the only piece of jewelry he still had from prior to the day we first met. He took it off and placed it around my neck. He kissed it and said that it was now for me to wear. He made me promise that Devin would eventually get his cross. As I was ready to reply, he stopped me abruptly in mid-sentence. He said, "Listen carefully. You need to understand how important this is to me. It was Devin that brought me to the cross. And it has to be Devin who gets mine. Don't worry... God will let you know when it's time for him to have it." What a powerful message that was for me to swallow. And yet, he was so correct in his words. Devin had been the Lord's tool in bringing us *both* to the cross. He was the bond we shared who added more meaning and purpose to our life together. And it was also the perfect way to tell me where he was going. This marked a beginning to our end.

The next day, pain increased, and conversation became less. Our closest church family gathered at the house on the following night. As odd as this may sound, it felt in our hearts like a going-away party. We sang the most Spirit-filled praise and worship together with our chaplain playing the piano more beautifully than ever before. My husband's eyes were as wide as huge silver dollars, flitting from one side of the room to the other. There was an intense presence of power felt by all. Throughout that night, the room was filled with angels. Although it would be some time before we spoke of this experience again, it had affected each of us profoundly.

During a break to regain our wind, the pastor sat at my husband's bedside and asked him what he was looking at. It was apparent that he was seeing something the rest of us were missing. And then, he blurted out, "It's Jesus. He's waiting to take me with Him. I see Him." It was not the kind of moment that stopped all activity but only rested on us as a simple, wonderful statement. Devin was so uplifted that he had been dancing incessantly around the room with excitement and joy. These were moments that have no other explanation apart from supernatural. They're only associated with people who are Christ-centered. And it is only through His love for us that we are able to get through such difficult times. It's by believing in an eternity with our Heavenly Father that we can rise up and be more than conquerors. It would also be the last night that my husband spoke again.

As a new day unfolded, the only importance it held was to comfort him from the pain his weary body was facing. Hospice made plans to spend the night with me as did one of my closest friends. Devin had been sleeping in our room as I remained on the couch beside my husband's hospital bed. It had become my battleground throughout the entirety of this war. I did not want him to suffer, and I trusted God would not let that happen. He had run his race. He was awaiting the finish line... to get his crown of victory. Our sweet Savior had a new body waiting for him that would never get tired and would never be sick again. He was already saved, and I knew that he would get to spend eternity not only with Jesus but with our two babies who had departed this earth before Devin's arrival. What more could one desire?

We tend to think that a person who leaves this world at a young age has not been given enough time to enjoy a full life. We get greedy and always want more moments with them. We think that our lives cannot go on without them, but they do… and will.

The Lord said that He would take care of Devin and me. And in one of our conversations, my husband stated that God had told him the same. Our lives are not our own, nor do we get to choose the length of our lives. Our family, children, and friends are only given to us by our Heavenly Father on loan. They were *never* ours to keep.

And so, in the early hours of the following morning, he left us behind. As I held his hand, I felt him drift away and into the Lord's arms. This may not be easy for some to understand, but it was a beautiful moment for me… to know where he was going. Nothing can satisfy one's soul more than the confidence of knowing that a loved one has gone to Heaven.

My heart was only saddened that I would now be all that Devin had. I knew that he had God but was not sure if there would come a day when he would deeply understand the significance of that. Communicating things he understood was still a huge milestone we had not yet achieved.

After our chaplain, coroner, and funeral home were called, Devin was just awakening. At first, I kept him in our bedroom to speak with him. I asked the Holy Spirit to guide me in what to say, and He delivered quite wonderfully… as usual. As we sat on the bed, I said, "Devin, Dad isn't sick anymore. God took away all his pain and suffering this morning. Do you remember when we agreed to let God do this His way?"

Devin replied, with his sweetest eyes, "Yes, Mom."

I told him that God's plan was different than the one we were hoping for.

And with that, he replied quite plainly, "I know, Mom. Dad... he went home... to Heaven." His little hand shot straight up in the air as he said the word, "home." My mouth then became utterly speechless.

When words finally came, it was, "Yes, Devin. He is home in Heaven now... with Jesus. But his tired, worn out body is still in the den. I need to ask you, Son, if you want to tell Dad's body 'goodbye'." I don't know why that came out as bluntly as it did, but I was on auto-pilot. I just let the Holy Spirit guide these words that were flowing so freely. I could not attempt doing it by myself. I told Devin, "Look... You don't have to do this. Mom will stay in this room with you for as long as you want. You don't have to do anything that makes you feel bad."

But, to my surprise, he insisted on going in there and telling his Daddy, "Goodbye."

As we walked into the room, he looked at me and smiled. The dog was already there, telling him "goodbye" in her own way. Our son ran over to the bed and crawled up next to him. He kissed him so tenderly and hugged his body as boldly as ever before. He said, "See ya, Dad." And with that, he returned to my side, expressionless, and told me, "All done."

We had to literally drag the dog away from him when they came from the funeral home. I took her and Devin back into the bedroom, and there we stayed until they left.

Shortly after, people came for the hospital bed and the rest of the gear that accompanied it. My friends were also arriving, little by little, to comfort us. As they helped me with completing the final details, I felt as if I, too, had left this world. There was an emptiness remaining that only

God could now fill. I could not think on my own anymore. I reacted to everything around me as if it were a dream. I only wanted to hold Devin constantly. I thought that he needed my hugs for comfort, but it was I who needed *his*. Although God's presence was there, He was not saying anything to me. This left a feeling of solitude that I did not know how to handle. The days ahead would be more uncertain, and if I dwelt long on them, I would eventually collapse.

I leaned on God to help me through every step of the funeral. His guidance in dealing with all the legal paperwork was also needed. There were so many things that had to be changed and issues to be addressed. Trusting the Lord was the *only* thing that got me through each day.

Life, now, was drastically different. Once you've shared a huge part of it as a team, without that partner, your identity becomes lost. You forget who that girl used to be before you became a couple and a family.

All I knew was that my responsibilities had doubled. I did not realize that, while my Heavenly Father gave no words of encouragement, He was already setting the scene for the new adventure ahead. He was placing specific people before me to help in all areas needed. Each and every day, He carried us, providing like the loving Father that He is.

His grace will always be sufficient. As I learned more about myself, He continued molding more of my character. I was not supposed to go back to being the girl I was. I had been blossoming into the creation that my Lord had intended for me to become. He was making a way of provision for both Devin and me daily. And during this period of change, my heart grew even closer to Him.

6

A Faithful Father

"A father to the fatherless, a defender of widows,
is God in His Holy dwelling."

—PSALM 68:5

With death, comes a new beginning. And with that new beginning, come seasons of change that shape and mold us considerably—if we will allow them to. I had no choice in the matter. I was as vulnerable as the child that Devin was, and I clung to Christ with all of my being. I continued to pray daily to my Lord. I asked Him about every decision before I made it. I also continued the prayers of healing over Devin, making him recite them as well. In time, we practically began thinking as one person. He was now memorizing the scriptures with me, and our sheets of paper—as decrepit as they were becoming—were not needed anymore. We chose to speak God's Word into our lives and remained persistent in doing so.

Devin began speaking better, clearer, and paid more attention to what I was saying to him than he had in the past. He was very much reliant on me as, now, Rosebud and I were the very center of his world. He rarely talked about his Dad except for stating the fact, "Dad... he died." It was as if he would shut off that emotion entirely. It would come forth from his mouth as simply as saying, "The sky is blue." Yet, in time, there would be a breaking point. He would have to face those built up emotions sooner or later. And I was clueless as to how I could help him. I was not even aware of the degree of emotions that he actually felt. You can pay a therapist to analyze your grief, but in Devin's case, if you cannot talk about that grief, how can anyone help?

I was enormously blessed in that I did not have to work. Investments and a clear head in the financial area of my life were also gifts with which God had equipped me. He not only put the right people in my path for guidance and growth, but He remarkably provided wisdom concerning the most important decisions I had to make. These decisions are never easy, nor do they feel comfortable at times. But we are all on a difficult journey of growth in the midst of the unknown.

Blind faith can be the hardest and most painful thing to rely on. It can make you doubt everything and tear at your insides in several directions. That's where prayer, keeping the Word alive in your life, and maintaining a personal relationship with our Lord and Savior become necessary tools throughout your life on earth. We are all different and exquisitely created, so there is not some fix-all solution for us to follow. It's an individualized plan that God has for each of us. It is one that is every bit as unique as our fingerprint. And it is only through His grace and mercy that we are able to approach the next day with newness, forgiveness, and strength. All we have to do is believe, ask for forgiveness, and receive.

We discover in this faith that our lives are not our own. The closer we lean in to God the more we desire to give back to Him and to others. In doing so, the more He will give to you and trust you to handle. But my plate was full, and I was not ready to take the challenge of added responsibility. On many days, I wanted to throw a pity party for myself. However, He would not allow me to stay there for long. The Lord would fill me with His presence when I stayed close to Him, and good things always happened. It felt as if rewards were being sent down from Heaven's throne.

We could not afford the special autism school that was quite a distance from our home. So, public schooling and special education was the path we stayed on. Things were beginning to work out in so many areas of our lives. My son was beginning to interact with more of his classmates and teachers. Not long after losing my husband, Devin's name came up on several lists for added support. God's timing was *always* impeccable. Although I felt like I was muddling through each day, people on the outside could see the incredible works that He was doing for us. I still had no idea what His plan was for my life, and I certainly didn't know what it would be for Devin.

Sometimes, we just need to focus on the day, or moment, at hand. Too much thinking and problem solving can be quite exhausting and will wear you thin every time.

Whenever my nature of "taking the bull by the horns" stepped in, it would be my worst enemy.

As I fought with myself in a desperate search of rediscovery, I failed to see that Devin was also fighting his own battle. His mood swings and unexpected actions would become so intense that we both ended up in tears by the end of each episode. Because of his lack of communication, I had no idea that he was experiencing severe torment within. His emotions were raging from the loss of his dad and the drastic changes that we both were facing. Finally, during a complete breakdown from both of us, he screamed as loudly as humanly possible and yelled, "Devin very mad! And sad! And hurts bad Momma."

I grabbed him and held him tightly. I told him that it was alright to feel these things. This was not from anything he did wrong. It was just a change that we were going through together. God was still holding on to both of us tightly. I explained that, no matter how tough this would get, we had our "Big Daddy" always watching over us. He would never allow the bad things to take over. We had each other, and that would become enough through time. As we sat on the floor in Devin's room, holding onto each other tightly, we both cried for hours, letting as much out as we could. This outburst became one of our greatest breakthroughs. It brought a cleansing to our spirits, minds, and bodies that we needed tremendously.

My son was now learning how valuable it was to communicate his feelings. He realized that it was like uncorking a bottle of pop that had been shaken up numerous times. This release of pressure was healing, and God's anointing was already upon us. The months to come revealed even more progress with Devin's speech. Although he was not using bigger sentences, he spoke what was on his mind. And the parroting was starting to be a thing of the past. There were still days when I felt as if we were backing up, but we were never regressing too far.

Trusting God was now a requisite because it was only me who had to carry out the role of both mom and dad. My handyman skills were becoming sharper. Devin and I were now learning new things together. We were growing and developing into the people our Lord wanted us to be. With the love and spiritual support of our church family, we stood even stronger on His Word. Life would never be the same. Nor would we.

Blessings came in every area of our lives. Protection and security were given by the Lord in anything we did. He guarded our hearts, home, family, and friends. His faithfulness was so constant that it would become overwhelming at times. There was nothing too big or too small for our Heavenly Father to handle.

But, as the first few years passed, I was becoming more comfortable with just getting by. This was never His intention, and again, change would come. Whether we wanted it or not, we would have more to endure and other things to learn. The Master Sculptor would have even more sharp edges to chip away.

Discipline in the midst of abundant love is the way that we are conformed into more-godly people. That is the way we become more Christ-like and driven with passion through the storms we face. And through these storms, we learn that it is Jesus who pulls us up for air between each huge wave.

Along with his other difficulties, the hardest thing I was still facing was teaching Devin how to answer "wh" questions. Reasoning was not a fan of autism, and I was clueless as to how I could help in this area. He was growing on the outside, yet on the inside, his mental abilities were still suppressed. I wondered if his mental growth would continue at a slow pace or possibly come to a sudden halt. This was a devastating thought to ponder, so I chose to leave it at the cross. I would not burden myself with God's plans for Devin. I felt like he already had a very special bond with Jesus. This was one that I could only hope to attain. Out of the blue, as he played in his own little world, a song would pour from his mouth to the Lord. It was as if he had access to Heaven whenever he wished, and I soaked up the sanctity in each of those encounters.

Although caring for Devin consumed much of my time, I still felt a deep desire to do God's work. I was finding my wings, so to speak, and trying to figure out in which direction He wanted me to go. But trying to force God's hand, by overthinking would only delay the process.

We were now receiving help from a government agency, which assisted with Devin's needs as much as my own. This started almost immediately after the news of my husband's cancer. Once again, it came in God's perfect timing. It provided the opportunity to learn more and get involved in ministry as well.

As I began working with the churches more, Devin was growing spiritually in a lifestyle pleasing to Christ. He was interacting in Vacation Bible School during the summer with many of the kids and adult volunteers. I was not only noticing a change in his behavior around others but also witnessing how he changed those around him. Once people are exposed to autism, they begin to see things differently. God does a work in those who become involved. Many of us receive blessings from the innocence and beauty of a spirit like his. Many times, I saw Devin reach out to complete strangers in church by giving a hug and kiss on the cheek. These were some of the things he did on his own accord and without any instruction. It was I who needed to lighten up more regarding his behavior.

As more people got involved in our lives, the more church outings we attended. Prayer meetings, in which we gathered to pray for the needs of others, were also a part of our regular routine. During these occasions, I noticed that signs and wonders occurred when Devin got involved with laying hands on someone in prayer. God was working powerfully through my son, and my doubts concerning his future were being reduced in size. Loud noises were becoming less bothersome with each passing day. Interaction with animals had become a beautiful part of his life. It was not that Devin began conforming to the ways of this world but that he was learning to appreciate God's creations, as intended. And during our car trips, whether to school or on long visits away, he insisted that Christian music be played. Although the portable DVD player was still a crutch for him, we occasionally put it aside for singing praise and worship to the Lord.

Devin was brought into this world as a Catholic and baptized as a baby. But we started going to non-denominational, community churches due to a powerful encounter with the Holy Spirit during our first visit. After leaving that Sunday, he could not stop saying, "Electric church,

Momma. That an electric church." And from that moment on, it was there that we settled in as our home church on Sundays (aka. "The Electric Church"). I had been baptized a second time by choice but never thought of the necessity of having him do the same. He was God's innocent child, and I knew in my heart that Heaven was his eternal home.

However, I had a vision that was quite different from anything I could imagine. In a dream, I saw my son getting baptized in a large tub of water. He was 12 years old in this vision. As I watched this, tears were streaming from my eyes. I had no idea what significance it held. I knew that he was now 10, and I could not see him requesting such a thing so soon. He was still quite afraid of dunking his head back in a bathtub of water. Anyway, it was just a dream at the time. If God was showing me something in advance, I would see it come to reality in His timing. I already trusted Him with everything, so things like this would be of no surprise. I saw miracles occurring around me almost daily. This would not be likely in a two-year timeframe but was definitely possible with God.

During a service at the racetrack church, our chaplain was giving a sermon from the *Book of Genesis*. He was discussing the encounter Jacob had with an angel of God as they had been wrestling all night and into the morning hours. Jacob refused to let the angel go until he was blessed. And so, the angel changed Jacob's name to Israel upon that request.

This particular sermon grabbed hold of Devin's attention. I don't know if the intensity of the two fighting drew him in or not, but it definitely made an impact. I had no idea that he was listening but noticed him sketching at a faster pace than normal in a notebook he often brought to church.

After the service, we went straight home. During the entire drive, Devin was fidgeting more than usual. Finally, he said, "Devin, he change name too, Mom."

I asked, "What? What are you talking about? Change your name? Your name is Devin. What do *you* want it to be?"

He responded, "It's 'Redeemed'. Mom, new name is 'Redeemed'. God says."

I thought I would wreck the car. My mouth had dropped wide open, and I was more speechless than ever before. All I could think of was the sermon about Jacob. Devin was not just taking it all in, but he had received the message in full depth. He was telling me in his own words that he had been changed like Jacob. And therefore, he was known by a different name than the one we gave him at birth. There were no words to describe what happened that night, but it was definitely a work of the Lord.

Time went on, and unusual things began occurring more frequently. As I stayed faithful to pray over Devin's needs as well as my own, I also began praying for the needs of others. While I was reading the Bible one day, I noticed a verse that hit a cord in me at once:

> Therefore confess your sins to each other and pray for each other so that **you** may be healed. The prayer of a righteous person is powerful and effective. (James 5:16)

Without even realizing it, this was exactly what I had been practicing. I had become a prayer warrior, not just so that Devin would be healed but because my heart was pulling me in that direction. A deep intensity rose up inside each time I prayed for someone. I also knew that God was giving gifts to me through each of these encounters. My instincts were telling me to exercise these gifts for His purposes. The hunger to gain more knowledge of Him became voracious. I read deeper into God's Word and was discovering the power that Jesus Christ had been talking about during His ministry with His disciples. I was tapping into the power of the Holy Spirit that had resided in me from the moment I first believed. More and more, I began to witness people experiencing miracles in their lives. These wonders brought me joy for those receiving them. But still, a place within me was anxiously waiting for Devin's miracles. I thought that my faithfulness would be enough to receive the things I was asking of God. Though, patience is not measured in our time but in the Lord's.

I continued to give thanks to God for all the wonderful things He had brought me through. I was truly grateful that we were taking steps forward… no matter how small they appeared to be.

But, as I waited on my Lord, the enemy was also waiting in the shadows. He is always ready to challenge your faith and works hard to steal your joy. He hates you with a passion. And once you give yourself to Christ, don't think that life will become a bed of roses, for it is then that the war will become harder, more personal, and more extreme. Paul warned us in the New Testament that we would be constantly pressed from every side. So, don't drop your guard, but be prepared for anything that lies ahead. Remember that it is never through our own strength that we overcome obstacles. It is only by His love, faithfulness, and grace that we persevere.

Pep talks are always much easier to speak than to live out. I try encouraging others but only through the trials that I have endured with Christ. Know that, when good results are achieved, trouble is never far behind. This would be part of my schooling to come. I wanted all the promises my Lord was waiting to give me, but there were still many issues to work on. I begged for wisdom, and my Father was helping me to gain it.

Through this next season, I was like a child in my understanding. I was blindsided with news that would take me to a whole new dimension.

All along, as I thought I was becoming smarter, I was really being sifted like wheat. I was about to be tested and tried even further because God knew exactly what I needed. His ways are so much higher than ours. We cannot begin to fathom the vastness of His purposes and plans for each of us. And although Devin had to endure the trials that awaited me, our Lord would be working on his needs as well. The things that appear unfair in our eyes are viewed quite differently through God's. When we have to walk through darkness, the enemy tries to change our mindset. He works diligently on planting seeds of fear in our thoughts.

As I was getting comfortable in my relationship with the Lord, another lesson in faith lay just around the corner. When it crept up from behind, I felt as if I was being pushed off the side of a ship. Unexpectedly, I started falling in slow motion, without knowing the danger that was below. To simply hit water would have been easy, but the bottom of my landing was filled with terrible things that would swallow me upon impact. The crocodiles and venomous snakes that were filling my mind consumed me with terror. Again, I started out with an ordinary, normal day that would lead to a pool of confusion.

7

IT'S A NEW SEASON

*"He changes times and seasons; He deposes kings
and raises up others. He gives wisdom to the wise
and knowledge to the discerning."*

—DANIEL 2:21

It was the third year since my husband's death that was
approaching, and I felt more aware of the woman I was
becoming in Christ. I felt anointed with blessings that were
overflowing, and the joy of the Lord was dwelling in my
heart. But then, as with every new season in our lives, some
are there for us to give and others to receive.

I had been taking good care of myself to be as healthy
as possible for Devin. I exercised, ate right, and got every
check-up required from my doctor. I thought that my health
was as good as it could possibly have been. But during my

annual tests, my mammogram came back showing something irregular. I was shocked. I had done self-examinations as well as those by my doctor. No lumps, soreness, pain, or unusual appearances were found. Surely, this had to be an error on the technician's part.

A more thorough diagnostic mammogram and a sonogram were then scheduled. As I watched the tech who performed the sonogram, I was able to see what she was viewing. A black mass was there, and I was numb watching her take pictures of it. I could not think straight. All that came from my mouth was, "Okay, what next?" Had I lost my mind? *What next?* Where did that come from?

As I got dressed, the technician called me to the corner of the room where a hospital phone was sitting. She said, "The doctor is on the phone and wants to speak to you about these tests."

Now, I went from numb to freaking out. How did a doctor get on the phone that fast with the results from my tests? A woman's voice was on the other end of the line. She said quite bluntly, "I am Dr. _____, and your tests show that there is a definite mass in your right breast, which appears to look cancerous. We need to do a biopsy and schedule that as soon as possible."

I replied, "What? Are you kidding me? And who are you again?"

I did not have a calendar in front of me, and I needed to seek better counsel than the voice I was now speaking to. Everything was going *way* too fast for me to absorb. Although we scheduled an appointment, I had to talk to God about this as well as my physician.

When the babysitter came to my house after picking up Devin from school, we prayed together, and I cried. I was still in a state of disbelief even though the hospital staff were quite convincing.

I planned a trip for us to see my mother on Valentine's weekend but decided to keep this news a secret until I was certain if there was anything to even worry about.

As I was returning home from our visit, my regular doctor called me. He said, "I got the reports back from the mammogram and sonogram. I want you to have a biopsy but not by just anyone at the hospital. I would like it to be performed by a surgeon that's a breast specialist." My girlfriend and I had just spoken minutes before that call. She told me about a doctor who was spoken highly of by many of her friends who had battled breast cancer. He was an actual breast surgeon. It was now beginning to appear to me that God was already in the midst of this situation. It was I who put *Him* on the back burner during this drama.

I called back my doctor's nurse and said that I wanted to see this particular breast man. She said that she already tried but could not get an appointment with him for quite some time, but this needed to be attended to as quickly as possible. I told her to give me a few minutes and that I would call her back. I was discouraged. Had God given up on me? Or, was this not the surgeon to choose? I called my friend back and told her the nurse's response. She immediately got off the phone with me and made a few calls of her own. In no more than 10 minutes, she had already gotten me an appointment with my "breast man from God". I thanked her, but most of all, I thanked God because He was right on time… again.

Tests and doctor visits were taking place so rapidly. They were giving me a very familiar feeling that left a sick, filthy taste in my mouth. We scheduled the biopsy to take place in his office, which made me feel more comfortable than in the hospital. I drove myself home soon afterward, crying because of the pain the entire way. I had no idea how worked up I was inside until then. The lump had a 50/50 chance of being malignant.

When I arrived home, I took some over-the-counter pain meds right away. I looked at my calendar, and the date of this biopsy looked all too familiar. I immediately dug up my husband's old records of his cancer diagnosis and reports. It had been exactly three years since he had his biopsy done. When the doctor called with the results, it was again on the same day that we were given my husband's results as well. Just as his came back malignant, so had mine. It was a different form of cancer but was terrible news nonetheless. So many emotions ran through me. And yet, he was so direct and to the point. He scheduled another appointment to speak with me about the next steps to take in this matter. And as I remained emotionless on the outside, I was screaming within, like a volcano ready to erupt.

The doctor's call came during an annual meeting we were having for Devin. All the service providers who managed his case were at our home, reviewing his progress reports. Although I took the call in my bedroom, I had to gather my composure in order to return to the meeting and finish it up. The monsoon raging within could not be suppressed much longer.

As soon as they left, I cried to the babysitter, who was not only a close spiritual friend but was also a big part of our "church" family. We prayed, and I declared that this lump would dissolve into nothing. I knew that, when we joined in prayer, supernatural things happened. But my feelings that were still part of me were fighting to declare residence. I felt more pain than anger toward God.

I had been to healing revivals prior to the biopsy and truly believed that God would heal me. I would even lay the Bible draped over my breast each night when I prayed, until sleep took over. But what I was asking for was not in His plan, and I felt deserted by my Heavenly Father. How could He allow the devil to get away with something so personal? Why was this happening on the same days that I went through all of this with my husband? How was I supposed to travel this road with Devin *again*? It felt so unfair, and I threw myself the biggest pity party that anyone possibly could. Yet, my Lord never left me. He had always been right there at my side. Though, I had not been looking into His eyes… only at the waves that were crashing around me.

My best friend came in for a few days after details were arranged. She took me to my surgery and cared for both Devin and I through the initial procedure. Upon completion, the lumpectomy was a success. The tumor that was removed had clean margins, which meant that they had removed all of it. The three lymph nodes that had also been removed came back benign. There was no indication that the cancer had spread.

Genetic testing had to be done to know what follow-up treatment to pursue. Those precautions are used to keep it from returning to any tissue in surrounding areas. My insurance did not cover those tests, but my God did. When I called the company to explain my income and situation, they processed the claim differently and wrote off the cost in full. Not only was this amazing, but the results came back showing that I wouldn't need chemotherapy.

Radiation to the entire breast was typically done with a lumpectomy, and the tests showed that I should also take hormone therapy as well. The radiation would be for 21 days, and the hormone pills would be taken daily for about five years. This was the plan. I always worked well with a plan. Put me in a direction, and tell me what to do. That was me.

But, the radiation was something I did not believe in. I hated the idea of chemo, which poured poison into your body. God eliminated that decision for me. However, the other treatments I faced would produce lasting side effects that I knew were not good. I took such good care of my body, and I could not grasp the idea of tearing it down through such means. The cancer had been removed, and the lymph nodes were clean. Yet still, I would have another walk before me that I dreaded. They told me that this radiation treatment would be necessary in order to stop any undetected cancer cells from surfacing. Statistics showed great results with this type of follow-up. But, I wanted a word from God to convince me that this was what I needed to do.

At a church meeting with elder pastors, I spoke to one in particular. As I explained to him what I was going through, I was sobbing profusely and could not stop trembling. I told him that I knew how Moses felt when God told him to lead His people out of Egypt. Moses insisted that he was not the one for the job. He tried to present a good argument: that he was too weak, a bad speaker, and definitely not leadership material. Well, so was I. I could not do His work like this. I didn't even believe in radiation. Why would He ask me to do this, considering all I had been through already? I could not understand how *this* could bring any good to anyone involved.

But that pastor spoke life and purpose into me. It was as if my Heavenly Father used his mouth to tell of the plans He had for me. He said,

> You are not your own. You are God's. He knows *exactly* where you need to be, and He is placing you exactly where *He* wants you to be. I don't know what God wants you to do, but He will guide you through this journey. Maybe it's to minister to other women there or for others to minister to you. But I *do* know that He is never wrong about where He puts you in this life. And He will never leave you... wherever you are in your walk with Him.

They all gathered around me, praying deeply from their hearts, and His anointing fell heavily upon me. I was renewed by the Spirit of the Lord, and my family in Christ was now walking with me in this calling.

Radiation started fairly quickly after my breast surgery. The first session was to prep me with markings that had to remain throughout the length of the treatments. Devin wanted to wash the ink off so badly that I had to watch to ensure he would not sneak up with a washcloth in hand. After my first treatment, I discovered what God's intentions were. I was a devoted prayer warrior, and this now became a new place for me to continue that work for Him. Throughout my weakness, I gained strength in the Lord. And as that strength grew, the enemy became quite bitter about the results.

I noticed a woman sitting near me who was having a very bad day. She was extremely irritable and in a great deal of pain. I walked over to her and asked if she would like me to pray over her. She agreed, and as the first two words came from my mouth, I lost my voice. It was as if the devil had seized my tongue. My voice had been hoarse prior to the radiation, but when I started to pray, no sound came out. I leaned closer to her ear, and I whispered that these prayers were coming from my heart and that was all that mattered.

She was crying as she said, "You know who's trying to stop this?"

I said, "Yes, I know. But my Lord is bigger, stronger, and more powerful than this mountain we are climbing. Believe that because He is here with us... right now."

I left the hospital that day feeling like "more than a conqueror" in Christ. He continued to walk with both Devin and I every step of the way.

By Day Three, my body was feeling horrible. I tasted metal in my mouth, and it was so strong that it smelled like it was coming from every pore of my body. My skin was getting pinker, but the Holy Spirit referred me to "aloe vera... from the plant." I asked the nurse if I could apply this to my skin. She said it would be fine just as long as I removed it before treatments.

On the weekends, I kept the aloe vera on constantly. My aloe plant provided all the leaves I needed to keep me from burning. By the end of my treatments, that breast was only a bit tanned. Amazingly, it never burned throughout.

However, my voice never returned. I could not speak at all, and the cancer doctors made an appointment for me to see an ENT for this problem. They insisted the radiation had nothing to do with it, but they were still concerned because I had recently battled breast cancer.

Everything went back into high speed once again as hormone therapy started just days after radiation ended. A trip to the ENT immediately followed and resulted in a scope that detected another problem. I now had a growth on my voice box, just between the true vocal cords at the base. It was approximately the size of a lima bean, and surgery was required to remove it. This was another blow to my body… and another step in blind faith. But I was getting weary. I just wanted to stay in bed most of the time. I could not talk on the phone, order food through a drive through, or even communicate with Devin. I used an electronic board to write down everything and depended on others to speak on my behalf. You don't realize how important your voice is until it's gone for quite a while. Urgent calls needed to be made constantly to doctors and insurance companies. This became more than frustrating. The hormone-therapy pills I took were making my throat drier and my mood swings extremely erratic. It became extremely difficult to get from one day to the next. But God carried me through each one triumphantly.

During these physical trials, the enemy came at me with full force. Major things repeatedly broke in the house. I was getting drained financially, mentally, and emotionally. I needed an entire air conditioner at the beginning of summer while doing radiation treatment. The home builder had not put a large enough unit in the house for its size. So, additional adjustments were made to compensate. The clothes dryer, hot water heater, microwave, house repairs, etc... these types of breaks happened almost daily. I was attacked constantly, but still I *never* gave up my faith. I thanked God for every victory in each encounter and knew that His faithfulness would prevail.

He was already helping Devin to grow in ways that I could never do on my own. My son and our dog both ran obediently to my side whenever I whistled for help. I was so thankful that Devin was terrific at reading and spelling. When I needed a voice, I would write down something for him to say for me. This was excellent practice in verbalizing complete, meaningful sentences. His sympathy during my anguish led him to help me with more chores. He would put away all the clean clothes that I folded. He picked up his dishes and mine when we finished eating. He even started feeding the dog when I simply pointed to the clock. My sweet Father never stopped showing me how much He loved me or how deeply He cared about even the smallest things in my life. Not only were we learning, trusting, and enduring in *His* strength, but we were examples of His greatness for others to witness.

Once the cancer treatments were completed, throat surgery was scheduled. This was even more painful than the breast surgery. Going down my throat to remove the growth had my entire mouth, gums, and tongue torn up severely. Swallowing burned, and my breathing even felt strained. I did everything I was told for as long as I was supposed to. But after weeks, my voice still had not returned. I was so miserable and completely spent.

The biopsy of the growth and tissue removed both came back benign. Although I was enormously thankful, something did not feel right. The ENT said that I would need a speech therapist to learn how to speak again, but she insisted that I was not healed enough to attempt that. Her advice was to seek another opinion before returning back to her office. It felt as if they were spinning me around in circles, and my other doctors were clueless. I decided to get all of the medical records from my ENT and from the hospital's notes of my surgery as well.

I found another throat specialist, who had been highly recommended, to do a follow up exam. He was a sweet man who was quite sympathetic to all that I had been through. He scoped me as was usually done… but with bad results. The growth had returned. It was about the same size as the previous nodule and in the same area. I started crying all over again. I could not do this anymore. I was maxed out. His report was not what I wanted to hear, and all patience evaporated. He told me to return in a couple of months and to try speaking as little as possible until then. Did he even realize how long it had been already? I asked quite bluntly, "Can this only be removed with surgery?"

He simply replied, "Yes."

Being so upset, I was about to reach out in desperation as never before… *openly*. As I continued to cry incessantly in that examining chair, I looked up to Heaven and said, "Do you hear him Jesus? Only You know the truth in my heart. I can't do this again. So, *You* need to eradicate this thing Yourself. *Please*, Lord?!"

That poor doctor did not know what to say. He heard my plea and knew there was nothing he could do to comfort me. He tried reassuring me that everything would be alright. "Just wait a couple more months, Honey, and we'll look at it then. Okay?"

But I knew what he knew. I understood the medical solution for my diagnosis. It was the same as the first ENT... only surgery could remove it. I left the room, and as I sat in my car still sobbing, I called the pastor I was closest to. I strained with all the voice I could muster and said,

> Look, this is not good... again. The growth returned. And I just sat in that doctor's chair, begging Jesus to remove it Himself. You have to be in agreement with me on this, because I can't do any more surgeries. I just can't. That man probably thinks I'm a nut, but I don't care. I *need* this miracle.

He stood with me in agreement and prayed over me deeply while still on the phone. Once again, God's peace covered me as more blind faith lay just ahead.

So, we waited. We tried to find patience in the middle of the chaos. As I quietly prayed that night—quietly, because I had no voice—I thanked God for something different this time. I thanked Him for what He was *about* to do in my life. I told Him that I trusted Him completely and that I knew how great He was. I knew it would take big faith to see big miracles. And nobody could do it better than my big

God. I asked Him to hold me tightly as I slept, believing in those miracles. I felt His peace permeate throughout me. That night had been more restful than ever before. I awoke with the same thoughts I had in the past regarding Devin, and the Lord then spoke into my heart, "I will make things possible in the middle of the impossible." Although I had no idea what His plan was, I knew He would come through.

One of God's miracles came within days of this encounter. Devin and I were at our racetrack church with people who prayed for my healing continually. I stayed faithful to the Lord in filling my son with as much of His Word as possible—no matter how badly I felt. After the sermon, our chaplain announced that he would be doing water baptisms the following week. Anyone who wished to get baptized was to speak to him after the service and bring a change of clothes the following week.

As we were about to leave, Devin grabbed my arm and said, "Momma, Devin get baptized. Whoosh down in the water... like Jesus."

I was astonished, first, that he was paying such close attention; and second, that he wanted to do as Jesus did. I asked him, "Why, Devin? You were baptized as a baby. Why do you want to do this?" I was not trying to discourage him by *any* means. I had to make sure he realized the purpose behind baptism. He needed to see that it was an important step in faith... not merely playing in water.

But then, what came from his mouth astounded me. He said, "Because Jesus is our brilliant Savior. He loves Devin... big, big. Devin, give *all* his life to Jesus."

Well, he already had me at "Brilliant Savior". The rest was just God, icing this beautiful cake before me. So, we walked over to the chaplain and asked him what he thought. Devin gave him the same reason that he had just given me. Our chaplain agreed without hesitation, with the most incredible smile painted across his face. He knew the vastness of this miracle that was transpiring before his eyes. He had witnessed the first steps in our walk with God through autism. It was he who first suggested we come to the church... even if Devin's behavior might become disruptive at the start. And so, Devin requested that it *had* to be him to do the baptism as this was our first church home. God was revealing His love, promises, and miraculous wonders in ways too extravagant to express.

The following week, as we prepared for this ritual, the enemy's fury was upon us. He carefully searched for loopholes to unravel the Lord's plans. Before church began, a storm rolled in like a hurricane tearing through our town. Lightning flashed across the sky in a foul manner, and we even lost power during the service. But God showed up... as always. We continued our worship and prayer in the dark without ceasing. Performing water baptisms outside would have been highly dangerous and appeared unlikely. But, we remained confident that our Father would turn things around.

At the end of the service, the skies cleared, and the lightning ceased. As we completed that sacred night, four children gave their lives to Jesus and were baptized as planned. Devin was not only prepared but more than ready. And when I thought that I had seen everything, God continued to show even more to me.

Weeks later, I was to meet with some women who were strong prayer warriors. They were going to pray for healing of my throat. I happened to arrive early and decided to visit the church secretary for a short while. As I waved to her, I wrote the craziest thing on my electronic communicating board. Here I was without a voice, and out of the blue, I asked her if they needed anyone for their annual Christmas musical.

She said, "Are you serious?"

I nodded and wrote down a big YES. I told her I could lip sync, mime, dance, do makeup, or whatever they needed. I could not talk, but I could do anything else. Being a quick learner, I would definitely figure it out. I didn't know at the time, but it was the last day for taking measurements. She quickly called for a girl to get my sizes. Being that I am small, she insisted there would be many possible ways they could use me. And so, with this ridiculous act of bravery, I was going to show my Lord that I was still faithful to do His work.

Shortly thereafter, I found my prayer companions. When I told them what I had done, we were all laughing hysterically. Although it was funny at first, a spark ignited soon after. They knew about huge leaps of faith and the powerful miracles they had witnessed through prayer. The Holy Spirit made His entrance and moved fluidly through each of us. They prayed diligently over me, believing that the powerful work of the Lord was mightier than anything the devil had up his sleeve. We left that room as if transformed. Something changed that day, but I was too drenched in His presence to know what it was.

Rehearsals were now starting for the musical, and I went faithfully. I knew that five months had passed without a voice, but I tried not to let it get me down. I was put in the choir for this production, and as completely absurd as it sounds, I felt like this was exactly where I needed to be. I found a wonderful, inner peace there. In the middle of the sopranos, altos, and tenors, it was like being with the angels of Heaven. I knew that I would get my voice back while amidst this very choir. It would surely be the perfect example of doing the "possible" in the middle of the impossible. And so again, my Father would respond as only He knew how. He would do the most amazing thing yet for the daughter He loved so tenderly. I was not anything special in my eyes or even to the rest of the world, but in His eyes, I was eternally priceless.

Ten days later, on the tenth day of the tenth month, my Jesus delivered. I awoke early at about five in the morning and had an uncomfortable feeling in the lower portion of my throat. I kept trying to clear it as gently as possible but had the taste of blood in my mouth. As I spit in the sink, blood *did* come out but not any more than that of a child losing a tooth.

Then, all of a sudden, this "thing" came up from my throat. It rolled over the base of my tongue and into my mouth. As I spit it into my hand, I was now gazing at this oblong, fleshy stone. It was quite hard and resembled a small jellybean. This was *it*! My miracle had just happened right before my eyes! More blood came into my mouth, and I quickly made a mixture of warm salt water to gargle. The bleeding stopped almost immediately. A dime was lying on the counter, and as I placed the growth beside it, I noticed it was half the size. I began taking pictures because all I wanted to do was share this wonder with everyone.

I ran in my bedroom immediately afterward and fell right to my knees. As I cried and prayed to my Lord, thanking Him for this incredible miracle, I realized that words were now coming out. It was not just my lips that were moving as before, but a sound was flowing as well. I could speak again, and all I wanted to do was sing beautiful love songs to my sweet Savior. All the trials and hardships I had been going through were now a distant past in my mind. I was looking directly into the light at the end of my tunnel, and that light was Jesus.

When something this big happens to you, rejoicing feels like the very least you can do to show gratitude. And grateful I was… with *all* of my heart. To witness my son's free choice of baptism was more than enough. But to experience such a supernatural event was beyond incredible. There was no operation required, doctors to see, or bills to pay for the greatest surgery ever performed. It could not get any better than that! Or, could it?

After hours of rejoicing, I did not know what to do with this miracle that lay on my countertop. I took a friend's advice by placing it in a Ziploc bag and throwing it in my freezer. I did not feel I needed to see the ENT any sooner than already planned. I continued practice in our Christmas play and waited patiently for the previously scheduled doctor appointment. When the day approached, I walked in as proud as a peacock… not for anything I had done but the wonderful thing my *God* had done for me. The nurses were blown away at the sight of this growth, and the physician's mouth was almost touching the floor. He was now anxious to scope my throat again as soon as possible. He looked it over carefully and said, "We have to get this tested. It's a good thing you kept it in the freezer." And with that, I replied, "Doc, you can dip it in gold and wear it around your neck if you'd like. I am positive that it's benign. My Jesus doesn't do *anything* halfway… only *perfectly*."

I knew his curiosity was making him anxious to see the proof. As he scoped my throat, he smiled and said, "There's nothing down there anymore. That's the same bugger I saw on your last visit. I read about this happening to a few people before but only in rare instances. However, this is the first growth that I ever actually *saw* that came out of any patient in this manner."

His nurse made sure to stop me on my way out. She told me, "You *do* know these things don't happen. Don't you?" I nodded *yes* as I hugged her and smiled. She knew that the "Master Physician" had taken this on personally. I no longer needed to see that ENT.

When I showed the pictures to my other doctors, they were just as amazed as he had been. All mouths dropped wide open, and they were pretty much speechless. I didn't have to explain what the Lord did. I only had to reveal it. We can't push others to believe; it's a choice they have to make on their own.

Throughout that year, I began seeing the ways of God more clearly than ever before. And it's through this level of clarity that true wisdom is gained.

8

LETTING GOD DO A WORK IN YOU

"For I am about to do something new. See, I have already begun! Do you not see it? I will make a pathway through the wilderness. I will create rivers in the dry wasteland."

—ISAIAH 43:19

Although we had experienced more miracles than I ever dreamed possible, we would still have to face more challenges ahead. Adolescence, to some degree, would be a thing of the past in no time. The pre-teen stage was already beginning, and puberty was approaching more quickly than I thought I was ready for. I worried about whether Devin would act out on any urges that his body was experiencing. It felt like communication had just started between us, yet time appeared to be running faster than before, and it felt too difficult to keep up. Devin's hormones were changing. His attitude was becoming more moody, and his growth rate was practically alarming. My son had already reached my size. He was stronger than me, and this could either work to my advantage or against it. Soon, he would be capable of overpowering me if it was his will. It was imperative that we have a deep understanding of the things that were appropriate and those that were not.

The gentle boy that stood before me was now becoming a young man with bodily changes he could not understand. How was I ever going to explain the developments of a young man when I had never experienced them myself?

It may have been convenient to have a man in my life at this time, but it was apparently not in God's timing. Typical men don't jump at the idea of getting involved with a woman, no matter how appealing she may seem, when her main objective is caring for a child with special needs. I did not have the luxury of relying on a weekend dad to help me care for my son. But I would be just fine. God had never let me down before, and it was not hard to trust Him now. He had helped me to grow all along, molding me into the person that *He* intended me to be. The work He had been doing in Devin had surpassed all my expectations. Fear *had* to be buried as a thing of the past.

At times, tempers would flare between us. We dealt with outbursts at home and at school, as well. Although suggested, I never believed in using drugs to keep a person emotionally stable. It may have been the answer in some cases, but I did not think it was for Devin. He had accomplished so much already through the work of the Lord. It would remain a final option for now. I always thought that, when something was restrained for long, it would finally reach a point of tension beyond control. Once that point arrived, the uncoiling might be too disturbing to manage. I was sticking with the guidance of the Holy Spirit. His wisdom was far greater than any I could fathom on my own. Unchartered waters would still lie before me. Only this time, I was not the same little girl anymore. I was maturing into a woman I only dreamed of becoming. And in knowing that God's ways are much higher than mine, I gained solid footing amidst all that arose.

I realized soon enough that the outbursts Devin was having had not all stemmed from his hormones. The school board in our district had done away with sensory rooms at the beginning of sixth grade. I was thankful that we were still receiving occupational therapy outside of the school due to a waiver program he received from our government. But this disturbed me for the others who were struggling. These kids were experiencing the same changes as Devin. The teens without special challenges are able to let off steam through sports and group activities that my son was not yet able to participate in. Pent-up energy needs some sort of outlet, and these "sensory stations" are crucial in allowing those with anxiety issues to release their anxiety in a more controlled manner. The activities in these rooms involve tools that help deal with individual issues. They allow the young people to relieve stress through hanging, swinging, rocking, or other exercises. This is very important for maintaining a healthy balance in their chemistry. Being left without this outlet during such life changes is completely absurd. But I was only one of many who were dealing with this lack of support.

Although I've heard many say, "Let go and let God", I could not find verses in the Bible to back that up literally. However, this is truly the way one deepens his or her relationship with God. There are many scriptures that tell about the Lord's goodness, faithfulness, love, mercy, and grace. These explain how He takes care of His children and keeps His promises. His Word is as real today as it has been throughout time, and it will *never* change. However, *we* can change despite what we've been through or what we've done. His power is limitless. His love is unfailing. His mercies are renewed every day. And, as believers in Christ, the Holy Spirit is available to us at all times. This is not a fantasy but a major truth in real Christianity. We are the same sort of people who lived during Biblical times. We are rebellious and unworthy. We mess up things in our lives just as foolishly as our ancestors did. We are history repeating itself. But, because of our inability to be sinless, God made a way for us through His only Son, Jesus.

I have no answers to give others based on science, statistics, or human reasoning. My testimony of these events that have transpired in my life is what actually happened. I am not a scholar, special needs teacher, or any type of doctor. I only started out as an ordinary woman in complete desperation, a simple person needing answers, guidance, and strength. Through my deep and desolate valleys, I called out to my Creator, and He answered. He picked up all of my scattered, broken pieces and made me whole once again. He rescued me from my depression, and His love changed my heart forever.

You see, these are the changes for which specialists have no concrete answers. They can only offer textbook explanations of what they have been taught. They can give medications that have been tested through the years, with clinical studies backing the results. These they'll prescribe for almost anything that ails you. The reasoning behind their methods is based on scientific principles.

Yet, when Jesus performs miracles in your life, you don't care about the statistics. You only focus on the end results that *you* know in your spirit are true. The joy that's found in a relationship with Christ will give you a high like nothing else can. It will make everything around you irrelevant.

Addictions cannot sustain you. Depending on others for your needs will always lead to disappointment. And trying to solve the impossible is merely a waste of time. But when one puts their hope in the Lord, He will answer triumphantly.

The most wonderful thing I have discovered during my walk with Jesus is that He chooses the simplest people to exhibit some of His greatest works. It is through *faith* that wondrous things take place. The results may not come instantly because it is *God's* plan that will be revealed... not ours. It's what starts the ball rolling and keeps up the momentum. And when we continue to believe, speaking His promises into our lives, bad situations turn around for the greater good of all.

Through my husband's fight with cancer, I had to believe that God was going to take care of both Devin and me, regardless of the results. This was scary, but the Lord provided a healthy portion of peace upon my requests. His

powerful intervention calmed the stormy seas that were trying to overcome me. When the same monster attacked me, I
had to trust that God would take care of Devin. This was my
most difficult mindset to maintain. I constantly thought that
my son would have no one without me. The visions of his
world, under those circumstances, were too devastating to
take in. With our bond growing stronger each day, he depended on me to always be there for him.

As my faith had been growing before this trial, the enemy tried to beat me down in every way possible. But my
Heavenly Father had been preparing me since the very beginning of my life. He knew me all too well. He set me apart
from the world and uniquely designed me with His own
hands. My Lord knew me long before I was formed in my
mother's womb. His plans for both Devin and I were only
beginning. This was just another chapter in our tour on
earth. A few more rough areas were being smoothed in my
character, and a deeper layer of trust covered the foundation previously set.

Devin's healing had already begun. The milestones he
reached during those years were enormous. As more faith
paved our path, greater miracles resulted. But while I asked
God to meet my son's needs, He was already working on
my own. I needed healing just as much as he did. The only
difference was that my obstacles were hidden within. Just
because the world may not recognize one's inadequacies
does not mean they don't exist. Devin and I are still works
in progress, and I am just fine with that. I know in my heart
that he will be able to live a full and independent life one
day. I speak it out loud over him continually. And through
faith, it *will* turn into reality.

I may not have the solution to your problem, but I *do* know who does. I may not be able to guide you down the correct path in your journey, but God can. No matter what you do, whether right or wrong, things can always change. That is where hope steps into your situation. It is the key that will unlock every door you face. Opening your mind to the possibilities that appear impossible is also a good place to start. It is where faith builds and walls of doubt are torn down. It is where you believe in something much bigger than yourself, a God who is all-loving, all-compassionate, and completely crazy about *you*. He will always be your best friend, gentle advisor, and greatest weapon in any battle you face. Only He can change the way you think and act. But you *must* ask Him to come into your life.

Does this mean that trouble won't be around every corner? Well, of course not. The closer you get to the Lord, the rougher the course becomes. You will have the devil at your heels, trying to trip you every step of the way. He knows that, through Christ, you are also an heir to the throne. Your inheritance is something he will never have. And although you will fall many times, God is always there to pick you up, dust you off, and encourage you to stay in the race with Him by your side. He will also equip you with all you need for the journey. That's a trainer that not only believes in you but died for you as well. You won't find anyone on this earth more loyal than that. So, stop looking in all the wrong places. It's really quite simple. The hardest part is to believe continually that His grace is sufficient.

When we exit the stage, everything we leave behind won't matter anymore. Living eternally with God will make your time on Earth seem like a speck of dust carried off into the wind. Sooner or later, we will all have to deal with the loss of loved ones, and some of those may even be our children. It is a myth to believe that they are supposed to outlive us. This seems only fair to ask, but life does not give us fair. The difficulties that we cannot understand will weigh us down tremendously if we choose to carry them.

The Lord tells us to take *His* yoke upon our shoulders in place of the one we continue to bear. Sometimes, this can be the hardest thing for us to do, but if you will ask for His help in carrying out that decision, He won't disappoint you. Because He gave this life to you, give your time to Him, at least. We never asked to come into this world. We were created by God Almighty. When you begin seeing that you are truly His and not your own, things take on new clarity. And because of that, we have no claim on other people. The ones He chooses to place in our lives and the children He blesses us with are only borrowed. We do not own them, and we'll never have the authority to choose how long they will be with us. As displeasing as this may sound, it is merely the truth.

So, how can we get to this place with God? How can we open up our hearts so freely to Him? Well, it has to start with a need. For some of us, it will come when we've hit rock bottom and are in complete desperation. It's when the shelf of options is empty. It will come when the world around you collapses and you're at the end of your rope. You may be dealing with emotional, physical, or spiritual pain at the time. But we all will get to that place, whether we choose to admit it to ourselves or not. When pride steps in, we convince ourselves to take control of the situations at hand. In those cases, we are only dragging along, trying to find a comfortable place to settle.

Muddling through a pool of slop is not living; it's merely floating around in shark-infested waters. This is complacency and was never the plan God had for you. He wants you to live a *full* life that is overflowing in abundance. He is not a God who condemns you but one with open arms to save you. He understands what you're feeling, the challenges you face, and all of your insecurities. He wants to rescue you from that ugly pit, renewing your mind and restoring your faith in Him. Also, your Heavenly Father wants to have a deep, personal relationship with each of His children, but the real question is, "Do you want that with Him?"

I have come to the place where I trust Him without limits. Before that, I was too weary to fight my battles alone. Among those dark valleys I walked through, I chose to follow the Master of the universe blindly. I wanted to know the Author and Finisher of my existence. I asked Him to come into my life as my only Lord and Savior. And because my Father is a gentleman, He would not rush in forcefully. That's just His nature. As I labored through the years, trying to fix things myself, God was patiently waiting for my invitation.

I longed for knowledge and to grow in wisdom so that I could comprehend His ways more deeply. I desired the ability to love others as greatly as my Lord loves me. I prayed for patience to deal with the anger that arose in many situations, and I wanted more than anything to pass these things on to my son. When I lacked the strength to overcome my sinful nature, God stepped in, providing a way of escape. This was not something I was capable of on my own. It would only transpire when He provided eyes to see, ears to hear, and a mind to fully understand Him. Only then could this possibility turn into reality.

I pray that this book has brought light into your life and hope to difficulties you may be facing. You are not alone in the struggles you battle. There are many brothers and sisters all over the world who need someone to speak life and possibilities into them. There are people who need to be inspired. They deserve to hear how powerful God really is. It's essential that we are aware of how deeply He loves us. In knowing this, you can then begin to love yourself. We are each valuable, priceless beings, perfectly created by the Most High. His plans for us are filled with goodness, and He offers forgiveness to all who ask for it, no matter what wrongs we have committed.

Aside from loving ourselves, we should love one another. When we build people up instead of tearing them apart with judgement, we display the image of Christ. This is *His* message to each of us. I have spoken boldly throughout these pages because I know what the Lord has done for both my son and I. There is no doubt in my mind or in my heart, and I will never be ashamed to confess these things to anyone. I can only pray that *you* will enter that glorious place with Him as I have.

In the following chapter, I have provided many of the verses of healing that I continue to speak over Devin, myself, and others. If you have already started a walk with God, I encourage you to speak out about His love. Share with others the things He is doing for you right now. Step out in faith, believe with all your heart, and trust in the Lord as never before. Take courage because the impossible is *always* possible with God. Then, you will be able to confidently share your testimony of His greatness with all those around you.

9

SCRIPTURES FOR HEALING

*"Every word of God proves true. He is a shield to
all who come to Him for protection."*

—PROVERBS 30:5

In this chapter, you will find many scriptures for healing
and restoration. Devin and I have prayed a multitude of
these daily over our own situations. They will bring results
to those who believe them. I encourage you to speak them
aloud so that you will hear the verses as they flow from your
mouth. This will allow them to settle deep into your heart
and spirit. We hope that, through your walk with God, they
will be as helpful to you as they have been for us.

Please note that all scriptures throughout this book
have been taken from the New Living Translation. However, feel free to use whatever translation makes you feel
more comfortable.

Psalm 6:2
"Have compassion on me, Lord, for I am weak. Heal me, Lord, for my bones are in agony."

Psalm 30:2
"O Lord my God, I cried to you for help, and You restored my health."

Psalm 41:3
"The Lord nurses them when they are sick and restores them to health."

Psalm 91:4
"He will cover you with His feathers. He will shelter you with His wings. His faithful promises are your armor and protection."

Psalm 91:14-15
"The Lord says, 'I will rescue those who love me. I will protect those who trust in My name. When they call on Me, I will answer; I will be with them in trouble. I will rescue and honor them.'"

Psalm 100:5
"For the Lord is good. His unfailing love continues forever, and His faithfulness continues to each generation."

Psalm 103:1-4
"Let all that I am praise the Lord; with my whole heart, I will praise His Holy name. Let all that I am praise the Lord; may I never forget the good things He does for me. He forgives all my sins and heals all my diseases. He redeems me from death and crowns me with love and tender mercies."

Psalm 107:13-14
"'Lord, help!' they cried in their trouble, and he saved them from their distress. He led them from the darkness and deepest gloom; he snapped their chains."

Psalm 107:20
"He sent out His word and healed them, snatching them from the door of death."

Psalm 138:8
"The Lord will work out His plans for my life – for Your faithful love, O Lord, endures forever. Do not abandon me, for You made me."

Psalm 139:5
"You go before me and follow me. You place Your hand of blessing on my head."

Psalm 145:19
"He grants the desires of those who fear Him; He hears their cries for help and rescues them."

Psalm 147:3
"He heals the brokenhearted and bandages their wounds."

Proverbs 3:8
"Then you will have healing for your body and strength for your bones."

Proverbs 4:20-22
"My child, pay attention to what I say. Listen carefully to My words. Do not lose sight of them. Let them penetrate deep into your heart, for they bring life to those who find them, and healing to their whole body."

Isaiah 53:5
"But He was pierced for our rebellion, crushed for our sins. He was beaten so we could be whole. He was whipped so we could be healed."

Isaiah 57:18-19
"'I have seen what they do, but I will heal them anyway! I will lead them. I will comfort those who mourn, bringing words of praise to their lips. May they have abundant peace, both near and far,' says the Lord, who heals them."

Jeremiah 17:14
"O Lord, if You heal me, I will be truly healed; if You save me, I will be truly saved. My praises are for You alone!"

Jeremiah 29:11-13
"'For I know the plans I have for you,' says the Lord. 'They are plans for good and not for disaster, to give you a future and a hope. In those days when you pray, I will listen. If you look for Me wholeheartedly, you will find Me.'"

Jeremiah 30:17
"'I will give you back your health and heal your wounds,' says the Lord. 'For you are called an outcast — Jerusalem for whom no one cares.'"

Matthew 14:27
"But Jesus spoke to them at once. 'Do not be afraid,' He said. 'Take courage. I am here!'"

Matthew 18:18-19
"'I tell you the truth, whatever you forbid on earth will be forbidden in Heaven, and whatever you permit on earth will be permitted in Heaven. I also tell you this: If two of you agree here on earth concerning anything you ask, My Father in Heaven will do it for you.'"

Matthew 19:26
"Jesus looked at them intently and said, 'Humanly speaking, it is impossible. But with God everything is possible.'"

Matthew 21:22
"You can pray for anything, and if you have faith, you will receive it."

Mark 11:22-24
"Then Jesus said to the disciples, 'Have faith in God. I tell you the truth, you can say to this mountain, 'May you be lifted up and thrown into the sea,' and it will happen. But you must really believe it will happen and have no doubt in your heart. I tell you, you can pray for anything, and if you believe that you've received it, it will be yours."

John 14:13
"You can ask for anything in My name, and I will do it, so that the Son can bring glory to the Father."

John 16:33

"I have told you all this so that you may have peace in Me. Here on earth you will have many trials and sorrows. But take heart, because I have overcome the world."

Romans 8:11

"The Spirit of God, who raised Jesus from the dead, lives in you. And just as God raised Christ Jesus from the dead, He will give life to your mortal bodies by the same Spirit living within you."

Romans 12:12

"Rejoice in our confident hope. Be patient in trouble, and keep on praying."

2 Corinthians 4:8-9

"We are pressed on every side by troubles, but we are not crushed. We are perplexed, but not driven to despair. We are hunted down, but never abandoned by God. We get knocked down, but we are not destroyed."

Ephesians 6:10-11

"A final word: Be strong in the Lord and in His mighty power. Put on all of God's armor so that you will be able to stand firm against all strategies of the devil."

Philippians 4:13

"For I can do everything through Christ, who gives me strength."

2 Thessalonians 3:3

"But the Lord is faithful; He will strengthen you and guard you from the evil one."

Hebrews 10:23
"Let us hold tightly without wavering to the hope we affirm, for God can be trusted to keep His promise."

Hebrews 10:35
"So do not throw away this confident trust in the Lord. Remember the great reward it brings you!"

Hebrews 13:8
"Jesus Christ is the same yesterday, today, and forever."

James 5:15-16
"Such a prayer offered in faith will heal the sick, and the Lord will make you well. And if you have committed any sins, you will be forgiven. Confess your sins to each other and pray for each other so that you may be healed. The earnest prayer of a righteous person has great power and produces wonderful results."

1 Peter 2:24
"He personally carried our sins in His body on the cross so that we can be dead to sin and live for what is right. By His wounds you are healed."

1 Peter 5:10
"In His kindness God called you to share in His eternal glory by means of Christ Jesus. So after you have suffered a little while, He will restore, support, and strengthen you, and He will place you on a firm foundation."

1 John 5:14-15
"And we are confident that He hears us whenever we ask for any-thing that pleases Him. And since we know He hears us when we make our requests, we also know that He will give us what we ask for."

Made in United States
Troutdale, OR
08/06/2024